"It has been declared in various ver~~sions~~  the windows into biblical r~~e~~ 'd not only with determining t translating, restating and c e value of illustrations. Illustr~~a~~ revelation in contemporary ~~......~~ portraits that aid the hearer and reader in a deeper understanding of God's Word. Brian Hunter has documented his ability to view life through sermonic spiritual eyes and allows the reader and hearer to see the invisible, grasp the intangible and understand the incomprehensible - all is the language of the world around us."

Bishop Kenneth C. Ulmer, DMin, PhD
Faithful Central Bible Church
Los Angeles, Ca.

God has certainly placed his hand on this work. The Illustrations are presented in the light of experience, they reveal truths that are much easier understood. May these illustrations be a blessing to many.

Pastor Willie L. Radcliff
Pastoral Coach and Mentor
Cypress, Ca.

In *Illustrations That Connect*, Pastor Brian Hunter demonstrates how preachers and speakers alike can use every day experiences to bring life to their messages. These illustrations range from the humorous to the serious but all designed to drive home essential truths. Use this resource to brighten, deepen and enliven your messages for all who hear!

Dr. Jaqueline A. Thompson
Asst. Pastor, Allen Temple Baptist Church
Oakland, Ca.

The Ministry of Jesus Christ is filled with Human Interest Stories called parables. In this creative book *Illustrations that connect*; Brian Hunter has applied this effective parabolic principle, through fresh illustrations and anecdotes which convey the teachings of the Bible to a 21st Century audience.

Bishop Kelly R. Woods
Lead Pastor Covenant Worship Center
Berkeley, Ca.

Like water is to Flowers so are illustrations to sermons. In this book Brian Hunter gives all speakers a never ending supply of real, refreshing stories that will make every talk just a bit Better. Read this and be blessed and helped!

Bishop Keith Clark
Word Assembly Church, CEO Words To Live By
Oakland, Ca.

Illustrations That Connect is amazing! and so needed. Every illustration is concise for easy reading, with an alphabetical index to easily locate illustrations for your subject and purpose. This book definitely has legs. A must read!

Jareem Gunter
Author of "The Man Book"
Fremont, Ca.

One of the most important aspects of a sermon, speech, or any other form of public speaking is the way the audience connects with what the speaker is saying. The only way this is done is with the use of literary illustrations. Not only do these illustrations connect the listener and the speaker, but they also emphasize the relevance of the message to the listener. In "Illustrations That Connect" Brian D. Hunter presents practical, yet important must have illustrations for anyone with the desire to bring their spoken or written material to life.

Rev. Erika Godfrey
Author of Single Ladies C.L.A. P.
Richmond, Ca.

Pastor Hunter has a definitive gift, giving us a rhema lens to look through during these hard times. Through Illustrations That Connect Hunter gives us a Relevant method, communicating a reliable gospel message to reach and connect with common people.

Anthony Perkins
Pastor, Harmony Baptist Church
Oakland, Ca.

Illustrations That Connect

By Brian D. Hunter
On the Verge Publishing Group

ISBN-13:978-1519944009
ISBN-10:1519944004

Website: briandhunter.org
Twitter: @briandhunter
Facebook: Brian D Hunter

ILLUSTRATIONS THAT CONNECT

By
Brian D. Hunter

Long Beach, California

DEDICATION

To my father, the late Elder Howard Earl Hunter, mere words cannot express the depth of my love and appreciation for you. Some of my fondest memories of you are watching you studying and reading for what seemed like hours. Preparing to lead and feed God's people. You embodied what a real man, husband, and father truly is. I thank you for protecting me by saying no to things I wanted to say yes to. Thank you for our family meetings, teaching me a healthy work ethic, our before dawn talks, and even your discipline. Though I hated some of those things then and couldn't understand, now that I am a man I cherish and appreciate them. Thank you. Your love, lessons and influence will live on through me.

To my mother, Etries Hunter, You have always had a quiet but steady strength. With that strength I have watched you maneuver and manage through various seasons in your life. Your strength has remained constant. You are a survivor. Thank you for your nurture, guidance, wisdom and always giving it to me straight. (Even when I didn't like what you said sometimes smile). As a man I still look to you, need you, respect you, and just want you to be proud of the man you have raised. I love you.

To my sister, Rashon Hunter, many of the illustrations in this book bring back memories of our childhood experiences together while growing up. I still draw from our experiences and use them to bring clarity and light to the gospel. The best is still yet to come for you! I love you.

To my children, Imanni, Imarra, and Imannul whom I have used so many times as illustrations and examples in my preaching.(Though they say "Daddy don't mention me in your sermon" I know they like it when I do!) Thank you for allowing me to use you as examples for the sake of helping someone Daddy loves you!

ACKNOWLEDGMENTS

To my late grandfather Supt. Lavell Thompson, some of my first memories of God and church were given and shared by you. With tears in my eyes as I write this, I remember having great pride sitting in the front seat with you. As you picked up most of the members of your church in your wood paneled station wagon. I remember "having church" in small dilapidated, leaky, and moldy storefronts. Watching you preach "out your coat" and would wait with anticipation to hear you say your famous preaching tagline "Y'all looking at me funny!" And though you never pastored hundreds, you were a true shepherd caring for and holding the people God gave you close to your heart. Though you didn't see many of the things you prayed for me come to fruition. Your labor and prayers were not in vain. I am what I am because of you.

To Pastor Willie Radcliff, I am so appreciative for the influence you have had in my life. Thank you for modeling, teaching, and instilling in me the importance of character, integrity, and a clean reputation as the foundation for being a good preacher. You taught me to "see" preaching in everything. Thank you for the opportunities you gave me to exercise my gift. It opened up and a unique ability to illustrate God's truth. Thank you for instilling in me the importance of a good study ethic. I still "burn the midnight oil." Thank you for all you invested in me, as I am now trying to pass this on to those committed to me.

TABLE OF CONTENTS

Introduction

"Can you read me a story, please?"

This is the request of children all over the world. Whether it's midday story time or at bedtime, nothing beats a good story. Oh, and children always want the books with pictures in them! Images and pictures that flow from words help to shape the imagination for better understanding.

Images have inundated our lives in a way like never before. Not only through the means of movies and videos, but especially now through social media. Facebook, Instagram, Snapchat, Twitter, YouTube, and online streaming have all taken the image to another place. On any smart phone or tablet you can access full length movies through Netflix or watch your favorites TV shows through mediums such as Hulu. We have become a society dependent on images.

Many of us remember to get directions, we either had to secure a map or the directions were given verbally. Now on just about every cell phone or tablet there is a GPS system. We literally speak or type in the destination or the address and directions are given. But have you noticed the directions given are not only spoken verbally, but they also give you diagrams with arrows of left, right, or a U turn? Even navigation systems use words and images.

Karl Barth is credited as saying we need the Bible in one hand and a newspaper in the other. It was his way of saying we need to engage timeless biblical truth with current, contemporary culture. As communicators, we ask people to listen through a means that almost seems archaic, through the means of imagery in our words, so that peoples' ears become eyes that they might see the truth that we are trying to convey.

Psychologists say that we have two "sides" to our brain: a left side and a right side. The left side is given to the abstract. It is the "left brain" that deals with things of a more cognitive and logical nature; things such as language, numbers, and scientific concepts. The "right brain" specializes in handling things that are creative, such as patterns, shapes, poetry, art, and music.

Our challenge as communicators is not only to employ our "left brain", but also to add flavor and creativity by using our "right brain". As we turn the listener's ears into eyes, we want them not only to hear the message but "see" the message as well.

We normally spend the week preparing to speak using commentaries, and timeless quotations. Employing the Hebrew and Greek language, mastering outlines, and hermeneutical principles. All of this information we grasp and understand using our "left brains". But the people we stand to speak to every week have been flooded by images and stories all week long. So the question then becomes do we "force" them to understand and receive the information through an abstract lens, or do we take the extra step in giving them a window to look out of to see the truth we are trying to convey?

We believe Jesus was a carpenter by trade. Carpentry is a left brain occupation, done by following exact measurements with numbers and figures. Although He was trained to use His left brain, Jesus was a master storyteller.

Though He was trained to use His left brain, when we hear Him teach, He employs His right brain. One out of every three lessons Jesus taught used imagery and stories.

To help His listeners understand a spiritual truth, Jesus employs the use of parables.

The word parable is derived from the word *paraballo*. The prefix "*para*" means "alongside" and "*ballo*" means to throw. A parable is throwing a (spiritual) truth alongside something familiar to aid in understanding something complex. For example, to help us understand how connected we are to Him, He says, "I am the vine, and you are the branches."

A parable starts out as a picture of something that is familiar and common, then moves to illustrate and make plain a deeper truth.

When Jesus said a "sower went out to sow" that was a familiar picture to his hearers. As He was teaching there may have been someone nearby in a field actually sowing seeds. The people he was talking to knew that some seeds would fall by the wayside. Others would be devoured by the birds. Still others would fall on stony ground, and others fell on good ground, took root, and began to grow. He used the seed as the Word, and the different types of soils as different conditions of the heart.

When Jesus said "I am the vine, and you are the branches" they could identify with this picture. They were very familiar with vineyards in that region, and knew that branches depended on the vine to live. But the longer we look at the picture, the more it becomes a mirror, and we ought to see ourselves. The mirror must then give way to the window so that our listeners see God and His truth and ultimately receive it.

The scripture is loaded with other examples of creative illustrations, pictures, and stories to help others see a particular truth.

In the Pentateuch, we see images such as: temptation is pictured as a wild beast waiting to pounce (Gen. 4:7). In Exodus, the Egyptian soldiers were thrown into the sea and sank to the bottom like a stone (Ex. 15:1,5). In Numbers, the land will swallow up the people, but the people can swallow up their enemies (Number 13:32,14:9). In Deuteronomy, the Lord carried Israel like a strong eagle (Debut. 32:10-11).

In the prophets and poetical books, images abound like: Stubborn sinners are like mules and horses (Ps. 32:9). The image of grass depicts the brevity of life (Ps. 90:5-6). Isaiah wrote, "Moab would be pushed into the manure and would have to swim through it" (Isa. 25:10-12). Jeremiah's ministry is compared to a destroyer, builder, planter, a city, pillar, and wall. Micah tries to find godly people but it's like looking for fruit after the harvest. Zechariah says we are the apple of God's eye (Zech. 2:8).

In Revelation, John says Jesus would have a voice like a trumpet (Rev. 1:10). Christ is mentioned as the lamb and the lion as Judah (Rev. 5:5, Rev. 6:16).

Nathan, King David's right hand man, used a parable about sheep to bring conviction and repentance to David, a former shepherd.

The bible will always be relevant because the bible is about people. We see ourselves in Aaron, making excuses for the golden calf; David, covering his sins and then later confessing with a broken heart; Peter, weeping bitterly in remorse; and Abraham, giving to God what was best and dearest to his heart. Illustrations help move us from the impersonal to the personal and bring light to what is already relevant.

You may think that you are not the creative type or that you don't have much of an imagination, but remember we are connected to a God who is creative and colorful.

Just look at the different animals, birds, flowers, etc. Look at their design, shape, and colors. Being made in his image we all have the capacity to be creative.

This book is designed not only to help you get your creative wheels rolling, but that you might learn to "see" illustrations everywhere you look, whether you are studying, preaching, writing, counseling, driving, or just chatting with friends. Learn how to engage your imagination and see spiritual truths and interesting parallels in everything we see and do.

ILLUSTRATIONS THAT CONNECT

In the following pages I have compiled a collection of effective and insightful illustrations. Many of which are from my own creativity and experience. I have used them all personally, so I know they connect effectively with an audience. I have included application tags at the end of each illustration. But feel free to use them in the way that works best for you.

1. Walmart Doors

One of my all-time favorite retail stores is Walmart. I love the prices and deals in Walmart. Real Walmart shoppers go in for one item and come out with a cart full of items. I remember taking a trip to Walmart with my daughter, and in her youthful excitement she ran ahead of me to the entrance. Much to her dismay as she stood in front of the door, the door did not swing open as usual.

She looked back and said, "Daddy, I think Walmart is closed! I am standing at the door and it is not opening." I said, "Oh? Well, let's stand there together and see what happens." I grabbed her hand and we stood on the entrance mat together, and the door flung wide open. Puzzled, she asked, "Why didn't it open when I stood there by myself?" I replied, "You don't have enough weight and influence for the door to open. But when you stand there with daddy, I have more weight and influence than you do, and I can cause doors to open that would never open for you." **Tags: Influence, Favor - Source: © Brian D. Hunter**

2. Don't Throw It Back

The late Dr. Howard Thurman tells the story of his grandmother, who lived next door to a lady who did not care for her at all. To prove her disdain for his grandmother, she would shovel chicken manure over the fence.

Her neighbor fell sick, and Dr. Thurman's grandmother went to the hospital to visit her, carrying a bouquet of flowers in her hand. As she walked in, her neighbor was shocked and surprised. "Why are you here? And where did you get those flowers? I know you can't afford flowers as beautiful as those." She replied, "Well, these flowers are really from you. Remember everyday you would shovel chicken manure in my yard in anger and spitefulness. When in fact all you were doing was fertilizing these fresh flowers." **Tags: Enemies, Forgiveness, Love - Source: Dr. Howard Thurman**

3. Perennials

I have never professed to have green thumb, but I have tried my hand at gardening. I planted flowers in my flowerbed known as perennials. Perennials possess very bright colors such as yellow and purple. I was proud of the colors that illuminated my yard.

One day to my shock and dismay, I came home and the flowers that once were so beautiful were now wilted and brown. Once, they had punctuated my yard with vibrant colors, but now they were about to be uprooted and discarded.

But just in the nick of time, my neighbor informed me that these were perennials. Underneath the soil they have a bulb. They go through a life cycle where during the colder months they "die" and it looks like they are wilted and dead. But don't count them out; leave them in the soil. When the season changes they will come back to life in full bloom, once again displaying their beautiful colors. **Tags: Patience, Endurance, Overcoming - Source: © Brian D. Hunter**

4. Skipping CD

I enjoy listening to music as I drive. Though I don't possess the gift to sing, I love to sing along with the music in the car. Every now and then I would hit a hard bump in the road and the CD would stop but I continued to sing. A few seconds later the music would come back on. Though I encountered a bump on the road, I never stopped singing. As we navigate down the road of life, it's easy to keep a praise on our lips when everything is going smooth. Ultimately we will all encounter some bumps in the road. Don't let the bumps in the road stop your praise.
Tags: Praise, Perseverance, Overcoming - Source: © Brian D. Hunter

5. Always Get a Receipt

One of the life lessons my father taught me was to always get a receipt after a purchase. The receipt was proof that a particular price had been paid for a particular item. So if there is ever a question regarding the purchase of an item or if the item needs to be returned or exchanged a receipt is always needed.

To the casual observer they see your progress, success, victories, healing, deliverance, praise, happiness, and joy. They have no idea the price you had to pay, the trials, ups and downs you have had to endure. So we ought to think twice when we are jealous and envious of someone. You never know the price that was paid. **Tags: Praise, Overcoming, Perseverance - Source: © Brian D. Hunter**

6. Riding the Roller Coaster

I love to ride roller coasters! I love the surprise and exhilaration of every twist, drop, and turn. The true sign of a real, seasoned roller coaster rider is that you are screaming at the top of your voice and you keep your arms up the whole ride. Through every up and down, through every twist and turn, a real roller coaster rider keeps their voice lifted and hands up. As life takes you through ups and downs, through twists and turns, we need to keep our voices lifted and hands up in praise.**Tags: Praise, Transitions - Source: © Brian D. Hunter**

7. Osama bin Laden

Under the Obama administration, the navy seals caught and killed one of the world's most wanted men: Osama bin Laden. Though we never saw a corpse as evidence that he was dead, we still believed it, based on the word we were given.
There are times we have to believe simply based on God's Word. Though we have not seen any tangible evidence we must hold on to His word and promise.   **Tags: Faith, God's Word - Source: © Brian D. Hunter**

8. "Iron" Mike Tyson

Prizefighter "Iron" Mike Tyson. was hailed as a knockout artist, knocking out his opponents in the first few minutes of the fight. He held the title as the Heavyweight Champion, but we really didn't know what he was made of until when he began taking some hard punches, and was even knocked down. We began to see just who he really was. He began fighting dirty, biting the ears off his opponents. Only after being knocked down did we see the man he really was. Being on "top" doesn't always reveal who we really are. It's only after taking some "punches" and even getting knocked down by life's circumstances that we are able to see who we really are. What is really on the inside often surfaces in times of hardship. **Tags: Endurance, Suffering, Strength - Source: © Brian D. Hunter**

9. The Value of Negatives

One of my all-time favorite Christmas gifts was a Kodak camera. I loved the state of the art, sleek rectangular design. I took great care of the camera, making sure I bought only quality film. I enjoyed "snapping" the 24 exposures of film. After I had exhausted all the exposures, I would drop off the film at Fotomat to be developed. In about three or four days the pictures would be ready for pick up.
When I received the pictures back, they were in an envelope that had two compartments. The bright, colorful pictures were always in the front and the negatives were in the back. The negatives, though they are dark and you can't really make out what the picture is, are very necessary. You cannot have the beautiful color pictures without the dark negatives. Furthermore, the negatives are always smaller and fewer than the actual pictures. We see and cherish the bright pictures in our lives, but never forget that if it wasn't for the negatives in our lives they could never produce the bright pictures. Remember our negatives are always smaller than the beautiful picture that God is developing in us. **Tags: Transformation, Growth - Source: © Brian D. Hunter**

10. The Shepherd of the 23rd Psalm

There is an old story told of a Sunday School promotion exercise where all the graduates were asked to recite the 23rd Psalm from memory. First up was a seven-year-old boy, and he began reciting the Psalm. He did it with no mistakes, fluid and articulate. Everyone was so proud of him. After he was finished, an elderly woman made her way slowly to the podium, and she began reciting the 23rd Psalm. As she began to recite it, the congregation became silent, hanging on to her every word. Tears began to flow from faces in the congregation as she spoke with power and conviction. Though they both quoted the same Psalm, the difference was the little boy knew the 23rd Psalm, but the elderly lady knew the Shepherd that was in the 23rd Psalm through years of experience with the Shepherd.
Tags: Knowledge - Source: Anonymous

11. The Answers are in the Book

Mathematics has never been one of my strengths. I struggled through most math classes in school. When my fifth grade teacher would assign homework there were always two groups of students: one group would be assigned the even numbered problems, and the other group the odd numbered problems.

I was always in the odd numbered group, and I would struggle for what seemed like hours with my math homework. I had a friend who shared the same difficulties as I did with math, but for some strange reason he would always get all the problems correct. I was baffled. He was no smarter than I was, but he aced the homework.

He shared a secret with me. He said, "The teacher knows we have trouble with the problems, but still wants us to succeed and build confidence in our math skills. So all the answers to the odd numbered problems are in the back of the book. If you are having trouble with a problem, you don't have to struggle, just look in the back of the book and the answer is there."

The Lord knows we will encounter problems and will be looking for answers. Instead of becoming overwhelmed and frustrated we ought to look in the Book to find the answers. The answers to our problem is already in the book. **Tags: Guidance, God's Word - Source: © Brian D. Hunter**

12. My Daddy Did the Work

Early on I was keenly aware of what my academic strengths were. Needless to say math was not one of them. My father would spend hours trying to help me understand math. One night we wrestled with long division for hours and for the life of me I couldn't grasp it. It started getting late, so my dad actually ended up working out the problems for me.

When I got to school the next day my teacher was shocked that I had every problem correct. So of course she wanted me to come up to the board and show the class how I got the answers. I was sweating and nervous because I didn't know how to do it, all I knew is that my father worked out the problems.

I had to admit to her and the entire class that I didn't solve the problems myself, but my daddy actually solved every problem. I said, "I am just presenting to you what he did, though I can't explain what he did."

When the problem is too complex, our heavenly Father takes over and develops answers on our behalf. Even when we try to explain how He did it, it is impossible, all we know is "Daddy" did all the work. **Tags: Favor, Problems - Source: © Brian D. Hunter**

13. A Lizard Never Loses Its Head

One of my childhood friends loved animals up close and personal. One day he captured a lizard in his hand. He lost control of the lizard and in his attempt to recapture it he made a colossal mistake. He grabbed the lizard by its tail and much to his surprise, the lizard's tail broke loose, and the lizard continued to run for its freedom. The lizard lost its tail but didn't lose its head. Though he may have lost a portion of his tail, the lizard never turned around to see what happened or complain. The lizard understood the portion of his tail that he lost would eventually grow back. Though we may lose some things from time to time (money, time, opportunity, etc.), we must remember ever to lose our head. **Tags: Restoration, Growth, Maturity - Source: © Brian D. Hunter**

14. Hot Tea

As a pastor, I constantly use my voice. I was told that hot tea, lemon, and honey were good for the throat. Being a purveyor of fine tea, I have discovered there are different kinds of tea drinkers. There are some people who are "dippers" and others who are "remainers". Dippers hold the tea bag in the hot water for a little bit and then take it out. They dip again and take it out. A constant in and out. Employing this method, the tea bag never releases its full favor. On the other end of the spectrum there are those who plunge the tea bag one time and leave it submerged in the hot water. As a result the full flavor is released. The tea bag changes the color and environment of the cup. Which will you be? One who is in and out of the "hot water" or one who will remain faithful even under hostile and adverse conditions. **Tags: Perseverance, Maturity, Growth - Source: © Brian D. Hunter**

15. Elevator Stuck!

During our summer vacations, my sister and I would explore the hotel we were staying in. We would locate the pool, sauna, weight room, etc. Of course we would play on the elevator. On one of our infamous elevator rides I decided to push all the buttons at the same time and as a result the elevator became stuck. I panicked and began pushing buttons, ringing the alarm but to no avail, the elevator was not moving. I was in a panic but my sister remained calm. She pointed out that there was a small door on the inside panel of the elevator. She opened up the panel and picked up a red phone which was located inside. The line was answered right away. My sister told the man on the line that the elevator had stopped and we were stuck inside. In a matter of seconds, the elevator jerked once and began making its way to the next floor. The elevator was stuck, preventing us from going to the next level. I didn't voice the concern myself, however my sister acted as my intercessor by calling up the man who could fix the problem and take us to another level. **Tags: Prayer, Intercession - Source: © Brian D. Hunter**

16. Weebles Wobble But They Don't Fall Down

One the greatest sensations of the 70s was a toy called a Weeble. I enjoyed singing the tagline "Weebles wobble but they won't fall down." You could hit it, punch it, slam it down on the ground, but regardless of how it was treated, a Weeble always bounced back up.
Later I discovered that each Weeble had a small weight on the bottom so that when knocked down the weight would help them bounce right back up.

We may be knocked down from time to time by the circumstances of life, but we are able to bounce back because we have the Holy Ghost on the inside that allows us to bounce back each and every time. **Tags: Endurance, Perseverance - Source: © Brian D. Hunter**

17. Calling 911

My daughter and I were watching a documentary about police officers on patrol. In distress, a lady called 911 emergency dispatch. She reached the dispatcher, but she was in so much distress, all she could do was scream and cry. She never stated the problem, she never gave her name, and she never gave her address. But within minutes the police were knocking at her door. My daughter was stunned and amazed. She asked, "How did the police know where she lived if she never told them?" I explained to her that anytime someone calls 911, the telephone number and the address are displayed on the dispatcher's screen so they know exactly where a person is even if they can't say it. If the police dispatcher can locate and help without knowing where the lady lived or what her problem was, then how much more is our God able to locate and help us even though we may not be able to articulate the problem?
Tags: Prayer, Intercession - Source: © Brian D. Hunter

18. I Made It to the Top of the Mountain

A group of mountain climbers set out to conquer a mountain. Among their ranks was a novice who was embarking on his first climb. For several hours they climbed. At last they reached the plateau they had set their sights on. Once they got to the top of the mountain the first time climber stood straight up with arms raised and yelled, "I did it"! As he celebrated his climbing accomplishment a strong gust of wind almost blew him off the mountaintop. The more experienced climbers explained to him that when you get to the top of a mountain you never stand straight up, but rather you drop to your knees to avoid being blown off the mountaintop. We should remember after climbing and reaching certain levels of success. We should never gloat in our own success, but rather be humbled knowing that we could have never have made it without God's help. **Tags: Worship, Trials, Endurance - Source: © Brian D. Hunter**

19. Football Lineman

Most professional football lineman are tall, big men. One would think that their success on the field is connected to their physique.   However, surprisingly the key to their success is not necessarily their height or strength, but how low they can get as they execute a hit. The lower a lineman gets, the easier it is to knock down his opponent.
Our success is never found in our arrogance and pride; depending on our own strength. But in how low and how humble we can be by depending on Him. Humble yourself under the mighty hand of God and in due time He will exalt you.
Tags: Humility - Source: © Brian D. Hunter

20. My Daddy is the Bus Driver

A little boy was standing in the middle of a city block for quite some time. An elderly man had been watching him and asked him, "What are you waiting for?" The boy answered, "I am waiting for the bus." The elderly gentleman said, "Well if you want to catch a bus, you have to wait at a bus stop. Buses only stop at bus stops." The little boy replied, "No, I am going to catch the bus right here." The elderly gentlemen retorted, "But son, a bus will not stop here. They only stop at designated bus stops." The little boy replied again, "No, I am going to continue waiting right here."
So the elderly gentleman gave up and began to walk away. All of a sudden he heard the screeching of bus tires. As the little boy stepped onto the bus he looked back over his shoulder and said, "My daddy is the bus driver and he will stop wherever I am standing." It may not make sense to others what God has instructed us to do, but our obedience will yield some great rewards. **Tags: Faith, Obedience - Source: Anonymous**

21. Butterfly in a Cocoon

A little boy had the pleasure of witnessing a butterfly attempting to break out of its cocoon. He noticed that the butterfly was really struggling to get out of the cocoon. So he had a bright idea, and decided to help the butterfly get free. He began to break and peel off the cocoon in an effort to end the butterfly's struggle. With the boy's help, when the butterfly was free from the cocoon, instead of flying to heights unknown he fell to the ground and eventually died. He failed to realize that as the butterfly struggles to get out of his cocoon, the butterfly is developing the strength and the ability to fly. The struggle is necessary. **Tags: Struggle, Overcoming, Faith - Source: Anonymous (used many different ways)**

22. My Monogramed, Wrinkled Shirts

I own a couple of shirts that have my initials monogrammed on the cuff. Though I normally have them dry cleaned, every now and then I have to wash and iron them. To get the wrinkles out I must apply heat and pressure.
I had to make sure as I went out in public that all the wrinkles were out and it was presentable. Since my name was on the shirt, the condition and the way it looked was a reflection of me. So I worked hard to get all the wrinkles out.
God will spend time getting the "wrinkles" out of our life because we are reflections of Him. His name is on our lives, so we must submit to the "smoothing out" process, which may involve heat and pressure. **Tags: Trials, Strength, Endurance - Source: © Brian D. Hunter**

23. Background Cell Phone Noise

Cell phones have changed the way we communicate. Though cell phones are considered advanced technology there is a major flaw; while talking on a cell phone, you may hear the background noise better than you can hear the person you are intending to talk to. The background noise drowns out the intended voice.

The enemy wants to ensure that God's voice is drowned out and the background noise of negativity and unbelief become louder than his voice. **Tags: God's Voice, Instruction, Communion Source: © Brian D. Hunter**

24. The Mother Giraffe

During an interesting animal documentary, I learned when a baby giraffe is born in the wild it immediately stands on its feet. Shockingly, the mother giraffe takes her long, strong neck and knocks the baby giraffe back down to the ground. The baby giraffe gets back up to its feet again, and again the mother knocks him down. With dogged determination and on wobbly legs, the baby giraffe gets back up again.

In disbelief, again I witnessed the mother giraffe knock the baby giraffe down. After several knock downs, the baby giraffe was able to stand sturdy and run with the rest of the herd. The mother giraffe's actions may be shocking but the mother knows there are predators who are waiting to devour her baby. Their legs need to be as strong and sturdy as possible to keep up with the herd. So every time the baby giraffe got knocked down, it strengthened him for the journey ahead.

God allows us to be knocked down, but it is really for our good. It increases our stamina and strength to prepare for the enemy and give us strength for the journey. **Tags: Sovereignty, Trials, Endurance - Source: © Brian D. Hunter**

25. The Glass Elevator

When one gets on a glass elevator you can see everything clear and distinctly on the ground floor. But as you elevate higher and higher, the things that are on the ground get smaller and smaller.

As you elevate your life in Christ the things and the desires of this world get smaller and smaller the higher you go. **Tags: Righteousness - Source: © Brian D. Hunter**

26. Walmart's Return Policy

I had to make a return at one of my favorite department stores. I had my original receipt and the original packaging with all the parts in the box. In front of me was a lady who had a doll that was not in its package. The doll's arm was hanging off; it was clearly used and damaged. I thought to myself, *They will never take that back in such terrible condition.* But much to my surprise they took the doll back in spite of the condition that it was in. That day I discovered something about Walmart's return policy. They took the doll back regardless of its condition because they affix a sticker on the product to remind them that the product is theirs, and no matter what the condition they will always take it back.

We serve a God who takes us back despite the condition. His name is connected to us, and because we are connected to him He is able to restore whatever the condition may be.

Tags: Restoration, Salvation, Redemption - Source: © Brian D. Hunter

27. Imanni Carrying My Books

I was studying at my desk and needed a book from a shelf in another room. I asked my then four-year-old daughter to go get it for me. I described the color and size, and she was off to get it for me. I knew it was a big book, but I thought she could handle it. As she was trying to bring it back to me I heard her straining and grunting under the weight and size of the book, yet she was trying her best to bring it to me. After hearing her struggle for a minute, I got up to help her. Though she was struggling with the book, I didn't grab it out of her hand. I just picked her up while she still held the book in her hand and brought her back to my desk. When our load is heavy and we are having a hard time managing, God may not take the load away but will strengthen and sustain us as we deal with it. **Tags: Burdens - Source: © Brian D. Hunter**

28. Kids Celebrating Target Visit

My children love going to Target. One day, I promised them that we were going to stop by Target. After hearing the promise of a Target visit they began to sing as children do, "We are going to Target! We are going to Target!" over and over. They had not made it to Target but they were already singing and celebrating the fact that they knew they were on the way. Though we have not arrived at the place God has promised or received what we have been waiting on, we still can praise and celebrate on our way. **Tags: Faith, Praise - Source: © Brian D. Hunter**

29. Paid Parking Meters

I live in the San Francisco Bay Area. Downtown San Francisco is one of the worst places to park. To find a parking space you have to have the patience of Job and the luck of the Irish. So I circled the block for what seemed like an eternity. Finally I caught someone coming out of a parking space. As I approached the meter I noticed that there was still over an hour left on the meter. As a result I didn't have to put any money in the meter. Someone had paid the price before me.
We all need someone to help us.
We must be grateful for the people who have paid the price and made sacrifices for us. Allowing us to experience and enjoy certain liberties and freedoms that we never had to pay for. Parents, teachers, coaches, and mentors who were pioneers paving the way for us. Remembering that Jesus Christ Himself paid the ultimate price for us at Calvary. We reap the benefits of reconciliation with the Father. **Tags: Sacrifice, Honor - Source: © Brian D. Hunter**

30. In Need of a "Spider"

One of my prized possessions as a boy was my own record player. Though I only had three 45s, I played them over and over as if it was the first time I had ever heard the record. To play a 45rpm record, you needed something known as a

"Spider" which was an adapter that helps the record remain in the center of the turntable. If you didn't possess the Spider, the record would not stay in the center and it would be impossible to play. We must always make sure that God remains at the center of our lives. **Tags: Humility, Trust - Source: © Brian D. Hunter**

31. Use Spray Starch

It is a fact that a good, hot iron and spray starch helps get the wrinkles out of clothes. When you spray starch from a can it makes that *ssshhhhh*! sound. I was ironing a shirt and using spray starch and I heard the familiar *sssshhhhh*! sound as I sprayed. But as I continued to iron I was not achieving the normal result; my shirt was still wrinkled. It was making the normal sound but achieving no results.

Sometimes we can do something so long that we don't even notice that it is not effective anymore. We are going through the motions and exerting energy but with no results. **Tags: Maturity, Growth, Pain - Source: © Brian D. Hunter**

32. Steven's Stuttering Problem

In elementary school we took turns reading out loud. I prided myself on being a good reader, and would anticipate my turn to read. After reading my paragraphs I loved to hear my teacher say that I received an "A" for the reading that day.

But there was another classmate of mine who had a stuttering problem and as he began to read I laughed at his stuttering. My teacher heard me laughing and became very angry. She said, "Brian, since you are laughing at your classmate, I'm going to give him another chance tomorrow, and I expect you to help him. I am going to erase your "A" and whatever grade he gets tomorrow, that's the grade you are going to get."

Even though we are successful, we must always find a way to help and not hinder. **Tags: Growth, Helping - Source: © Brian D. Hunter**

33. Ranch Dressing

I love real buttermilk ranch dressing. Ranch dressing on salad, on french fries, on baked potatoes, and even buffalo wings. I love real buttermilk ranch dressing! Though I love buttermilk ranch dressing, I detest one of its main ingredients: buttermilk! I detest the smell and texture of it.

Though I would never drink buttermilk by itself, when it is mixed with the other ingredients it is a wonderful condiment.

We may not like the individual problems that we encounter, but when we allow God to mix it in with the ups and downs, successes and defeats, we ultimately see how all - not just one, but all - things are working together for our good.

Tags: Growth, Maturity - Source: © Brian D. Hunter

34. Grandmother's Quilts

My grandmother was an accomplished seamstress. As a seamstress, she would cut away fabric to form a pattern. The pieces that she cut away she called remnants. They looked like scraps fit for the trash to me. But instead of throwing away the scraps she would collect and save them. Believe it or not, from those scraps she could make an entire quilt. As she made the quilt it had two sides; one side looked like a hodgepodge mess, but the other side looked like a tapestry masterpiece. The side you looked at defined your perspective and reaction.

Depending on how you look at life, sometimes it can look like a hodgepodge mess. But other times, if we look at the other side it can look like it's all together, neatly arranged.

Tags: Trust, Maturity - Source: © Brian D. Hunter

35. Credit Union Doors

Upon entering my credit union to transact some business, I had to walk through a peculiar corridor. I walked into the door only to find another door in front of me. I tried to push the other door open and it would not budge. But I noticed as the first door closed behind me then immediately the door in front of me opened. I couldn't go forward until the door behind me had closed completely.Before we can move forward we have to close the door to our past, allowing the door of our future to open so we can move forward. **Tags: Past - Source: © Brian D. Hunter**

36. I Left a Note

A little girl decided to get up early and fix breakfast for her mother and father. She spent quite some time banging pots, mixing ingredients, etc. When her father finally came into the kitchen it was a mess! But the little girl asked him to read the note on the kitchen counter which read: I know things seem like they are a mess now, but I'm working on something.
Life can seem a mess sometimes, but God's word assures that in the midst of the mess, He leaves us a note that He is working on something. **Tags: Promises, Bible - Source: © Brian D. Hunter**

37. Rollercoaster and Paige

I never will forget the love of my life in fifth grade. Her name was Paige. I remember her vividly. Big, shiny afro, soft, smooth skin, bangle bracelets on her wrist, and she always smelled like cinnamon. Our fifth grade class went to a nearby amusement park, and I had the privilege of having Paige as my girlfriend for the day. I wasn't content with us just walking together - I wanted to hold her hand, but I could not figure out a way to get her close enough to do so.
We got on our first roller coaster together, she sat on her side and I sat on mine. Still praying for her to be close to me, the Lord answered my prayer. As the roller coaster began to make twists and turns, the centrifugal force began to work to my advantage. Paige just slid right over to me! If it wasn't for the twists and turns we would have never gotten so close.
God will use the twists and turns and the ups and downs of life to bring us closer to him. **Tags: God, Dependence - Source Brian D. Hunter**

38. Imanni's Tricycle

When my oldest daughter, Imanni, was a little girl she loved to ride her tricycle. She didn't know how to pedal yet so she would just put her feet on the pedals and hands on the handlebars. Luckily I did not have to bend over to push her, because there was long steering handle attached to the back of the tricycle and I could walk upright and push the tricycle.
My daughter thought because she had her hands on the handlebars she was really steering and determining where she was going. She that she was really controlling the pace because she had her feet on the pedals. But because I had the steering handle behind her I controlled everything. It appeared to her that she was in control, but in reality I was controlling everything. It may look and feel like we are in control, but behind the scenes God is still in complete control. **Tags: Guidance - Source: ©
Brian D. Hunter**

39. My Wisdom Tooth

I admit that visiting the dentist is not on the top of my list. The sound of the instruments grinding is not one of my favorite sounds to hear. I was having tremendous pain with one of my teeth, and I kept trying to medicate that pain with ibuprofen, but to no avail. The pain was relentless and I had to go to the dentist. It was decided that my wisdom tooth needed to be pulled. The dentist began to numb the tooth and made his first attempt to pull it out. Yet I could still feel tremendous pain. He administered more anesthesia and made another attempt. I could still feel the pain. He gave me more anesthetic and made yet another attempt. Still the pain was unbearable. He couldn't understand why I still felt pain; after all his attempts the tooth was very numb. What he discovered was that the tooth was so infected that it was blocking the anesthesia. There may be areas of our lives that can become so "infected" that the Word of God even has problems penetrating the areas where we need help the most. **Tags: Maturity, Sin, God's Word - Source: © Brian
D. Hunter**

40. Imannul's Kite

My son and I set out one Saturday to fly a kite. He chose a box kite. I only had experience putting together the normal, conventional diamond kite. The box kite was a little different. It had intricate design, multiple pieces, and I actually had to read the directions. What I thought would be done easily and quick was time consuming and meticulous. All the while my son kept asking, "Is it ready yet?" to which I responded by saying very politely, "No, almost." More time would go by and he would ask again, "Is the kite ready yet?" Getting a little annoyed now because of my frustration in trying to put the kite together, I now replied, "Not yet! I will tell you when."
All the while I am working, sweating, reading the directions, redoing things I thought were right. All the while he is skipping, jumping, and singing and never asked if he could help me. He let me handle it and kept asking was it ready yet? When I finished he had no idea what it took to put it together, but he flew the kite high in the sky with a smile on his face.
While God is working some things out on our behalf, we ought to let Him do the work and follow the example of my son; singing praise with anticipation while He works. **Tags: Trust, Maturity - Source: © Brian D. Hunter**

41. Driving by the Book

In California there is a stretch of highway called Highway 5. Highway 5 is a flat highway running through long stretches of agricultural fields. Although there are many rest stops and gas stations on Highway 5 they are stretched out over long distances.
I was traveling Highway 5 with a friend of mine and we made a stop and I recommended that we get gas, but he insisted that we didn't need to. So we got back on the road and after about fifteen minutes on the road the gas light came on. I became very nervous because the next gas station wasn't at least for another twenty-five miles, and there aren't any emergency call boxes on Highway 5. So I began to panic because I didn't want to run out

of gas. He suggested that I grab the owner's manual and see just how far we could go once the gas light came on. I discovered that we could go thirty-five miles after the gas warning light came on. Though we didn't know just how far we could go, the manual assured us that we could go a little further and that we were going to make it.

Just when you think that you cannot go any further and you are about to "run out of gas" the Bible, assures us that we can go a little while longer and we will make it! **Tags: God's Word - Source: © Brian D. Hunter**

42. All That Hair

Years ago I was dating a young lady who wore her hair very short. I remember dropping her off at the beauty salon and upon picking her up, as she walked to the car I didn't even recognize her because now she had long hair to the middle of her back. She went in with hardly any hair but came out with long, black locks. Of course in my amazement, I enquired as to how this happened. She explained to me that she got what is called a weave. What I learned is for a weave to be successful you have to have enough hair for the beautician to grab in between her fingers. The beautician then takes synthetic hair and weaves it into your real hair. If the beautician is good you can't tell where the real hair and fake hair is weaved. But all she needs is just a little bit to start with and she can do wonders.

No matter what we may have lost or feel we don't have, God can take what little bit we may possess and add to it. He can add to it and make it better.   **Tags: Growth, Maturity, Change - Source: © Brian D. Hunter**

43. Stand Still!

Though I am terribly afraid of snakes, I am intrigued by their habits and characteristics in the wild. I learned a great deal about snakes from the late Steve Irwin, better known as the "Crocodile Hunter". He instructs us never to run if you encounter a snake. As difficult as it may be, stand completely still. He says snakes only strike at objects that are moving.

All of us have "snakes" in our lives. Some "snakes" come in the form of enemies, even friends or colleagues. As long as we are standing still, our "snakes" really don't manifest themselves though they are all around. It is only when we begin to make progress and move forward, pursuing dreams and goals, that they manifest themselves, trying to impede our progress. **Tags: Vision, Enemies - Source: © Brian D. Hunter**

44. Snakes Don't Have Ears

Steve Irwin, the late, great zoologist, taught me another valuable lesson regarding snakes. He informed me that snakes don't have ears, but rather they use their forked tongues as "ears" to sense what is around them.

When he pointed that out I had to look twice because in all these years I guess I never really paid much attention. But he is right; they don't have ears. So they really can't hear.

You know you are dealing with a "snake" in your life because no matter how much you talk they don't hear you. "I told you I don't like that," or "I have told you time and time again I don't like to be treated like that." Or for leaders, they don't hear or see your vision. They aren't hearing you because snakes don't have ears. **Tags: Friendship, Vision - Source: © Brian D. Hunter**

45. Snakes are Cold-Blooded

It is a fact that snakes are cold blooded animals. They are looking for warmth and heat to sun in. They cannot make heat themselves, so they depend on the heat from another source to keep them warm.

Be careful of those who don't have their own "sun"; their own dreams and goals. They will try to warm themselves from your "sun". **Tags: Friendship, Enemies - Source: © Brian D. Hunter**

46. Apes vs. Duck

I love watching documentaries that depict animals in their natural habitat. One documentary highlighted both apes and waterbirds in their natural habitat. Both animals lived and thrived in trees, and both lived near water. Though they were both exposed to water, they each had a very different reaction to water. The ape was terrified of water and stayed as far away as he could from it. But the duck thrived in water. What was the difference? Though they both were exposed to the same elements, the duck was built and equipped for the water and the ape simply was not. So the duck thrived in an environment that would ultimately take the ape under.

As believers we may be in the same environment as others, but we can thrive in environments where others may be taken under. We may be equipped to handle an environment that others simply cannot. Moses and Joseph were both in Egypt; Egypt was a burden to Moses but Joseph thrived in Egypt.
Tags: Perseverance - Source: © Brian D. Hunter

47. Lights in Dubai

A friend of mine took his dream vacation in Dubai at a five star resort. He thoroughly enjoyed himself and had the time of his life. But something really threw him off.

In the five star resort every so often the lights would flicker as if they were going to go out. He discovered that because of where the resort was, electricity was hard to maintain. When the lights flicker they are really on the verge of going out, but there is generator in the basement of the hotel that kicks in just before the lights go out.

There are times when it looks like we may flicker out and give up because of the experience of what we may be going through. But because the Holy Spirit dwells on the inside, even when we want to give up, He gives us the strength to allow us to stand and not give up. **Tags: Perseverance, Maturity - Source: © Brian D. Hunter**

48. Flour, Plate, Ball

A scientist climbed to a lofty height to look over a skyscraper banister. He wanted to see how different things responded to being dropped from the same height.

He dropped a plate and as soon as it hit the ground it shattered into a million pieces. He then dropped a bag of flour and it hit the ground with a loud *thud!* and just laid there. He then dropped a ball and it bounced back up and down several times before coming to a stop. They were each dropped from the same height but each had a different result as they landed. Each item responded to being dropped based on what was on the inside of them and what they were made of.

We may encounter the same problems and circumstances as someone else. The circumstance does not matter. What matters is how we respond to the circumstance. We can fall to pieces like that plate, lay dead as the bag of flour, or we can bounce back like that ball from each and every circumstance. Because we have the Holy Ghost dwelling on the inside we have what it takes to bounce back every time. There is a classic spiritual song that says, "There is something within that holds the reins, something within that banishes pain, something within I cannot explain. All I know is there is something within." **Tags: Perspective, Problems - Source: Anonymous**

49. It Only Takes One Man

Vince Lombardi undoubtedly will go down as one of the best coaches in football history. Upon taking the helm of the Green Bay Packers, they had come off a 0-11 losing streak. After taking leadership of the team, they never had another losing season. They went on to be Super Bowl champions time and time over. The influence of one man turned everything around. Sometimes the influence of one person in our lives can turn everything around. **Tags: Influence - Source: © Brian D. Hunter**

50. My Father Made Sure I Lost

In my early teens I discovered I had a gift for running track. I became so good that I never lost a race from seventh grade to my sophomore year in high school. I didn't know what it meant to lose. With that kind of winning streak, I became very arrogant and cocky. My dad admonished me time and time again to remain humble but to no avail; I remained cocky as ever.

So my dad decided to teach me a lesson. I was running on the Junior Varsity team, and my dad asked my coach to allow me to run one meet at the Varsity level. In my arrogance, I surmised that it really didn't matter what level it was, I was going to win. I entered the race overconfident as in times past. As the race transpired I found myself slipping behind. At first by just a little and then by a lot! I could literally see the back of my opponents as they left me in the dust. I ran as fast as I could but fell further behind. I was embarrassed as I came in a miserable sixth place.

After the race I literally had a temper tantrum melt down. My attitude was terrible! My dad came out to the infield to straighten me out. He informs me that he told the coach to put me in a varsity race, and I demanded (gently of course) why he would do such a thing? He replied that I needed to know how to handle myself not just as a winner, but I also needed to know how to handle my losses. He said, "Son, you learn more from your losses than you do from your wins." After that, needless to say I was so much more humble and learned how to respond to my losses.

Our Heavenly Father wants to make sure we are balanced; that we would know how to handle good success, but also know how to handle and balance disappointments and losses. On purpose he gives us both. Paul says, "I have learned how to both be abased and abound. How to be in full and how to be in want."
Tags: Perspective, Growth, Maturity - Source: © Brian D. Hunter

51. Thankful for the Storm

A young woman was kidnapped from a grocery store parking lot, pulled into a van, and driven to a remote location in the woods. She was beaten and raped, wrapped in duct tape from head to toe and thrown in a ditch to die.

To make matters worse, as she was lying in the ditch trapped in duct tape, it began to rain.

Fortunately she survived the ordeal. After she was found and rescued they interviewed her and asked how she survived. She recounted how she was trapped in duct tape and she could not move or scream and it began to rain. At first she thought that it couldn't get any worse than what it was and now it's raining? But the rain was what actually saved her life; it began to loosen the duct tape which allowed her to free her hands and feet to get help. So the storm actually saved her life.

Though it may not seem like it, the storms of our lives can actually work to our advantage. What seems like a problem can really be a stepping stone that will work for our good. **Tags: Problems, Deliverance, Perspective - Source: © Brian D. Hunter**

52. Pop Up Blockers

It can be very frustrating to be working on a computer project, and all of sudden out of nowhere an annoying ad pops up. Pop ups are a nuisance because they pop up right in the middle of the screen covering and blocking the very thing I am working on. The remedy is a pop up blocker; a software program that prevents any unexpected pop ups from coming onto your screen thereby preventing your work. Unbeknownst to us at times God has blocked things in our life to limit our distractions and help us to be as productive as we can. **Tags: Protection**

53. Shrek the Sheep

New Zealand news headlines tells the story of a Shrek the sheep, who became famous several years ago when he was found after hiding out in caves for six years. Of course, during this time his fleece grew without anyone there to shear (shave) it. When he was finally found and shaved, his fleece weighed an amazing sixty pounds. Most sheep have fleece weighing just under ten pounds, with the exception usually reaching fifteen pounds, maximum.

For six years, Shrek carried six times the regular weight of his fleece, simply because he was away from his shepherd. When Shrek was found, a professional sheep shearer took care of Shrek's fleece in twenty-eight minutes. Shrek's sixty-pound fleece was finally removed. All it took was coming home to his shepherd.

This reminds me of John 10 when Jesus compares Himself to a shepherd, and His followers are His sheep. Shrek is much like a person who knows Jesus Christ but has wandered. If we avoid Christ's constant refining of our character, we're going to accumulate extra weight in this world—a weight we don't have to bear. Christ can lift the burdens we carry, if only we stop hiding. He can shave off our 'fleece'—that is, our self-imposed burdens brought about by wandering from our Good Shepherd.

Tags: Dependence

54. The NASA Take Off

Witnessing a space shuttle take off is literally breathtaking. As it lifts off the engines are spewing fire and combustion as it is climbs higher and higher. As it moves into outer space and reaches a certain altitude certain things begin to fall off the spacecraft as well. The higher it goes the lighter it becomes. It cannot have certain limitations and weight as it reaches new heights. As we go higher reaching different levels and heights in our lives, there are people and other limitations that must be taken off if we are to soar to the heights that we are destined.

Tags: Growth - Source: © Brian D. Hunter

55. Aliyah Houghton

On August 25, 2001 the world was shocked to hear that the young R&B singing sensation known as Aliyah had been killed in an airplane crash. In a hurry to get back to the U.S. from the Bahamas the plane was overloaded with crew and equipment. Upon takeoff the plane was too heavy to get the proper liftoff and crashed to the ground. The plane never reached its destined altitude because of its weight.
We must be careful that we are not overloaded by people, thoughts, and our own limitations that we never reach the destination we were intended to reach. **Tags: Burdens - Source: © Brian D. Hunter**

56. Astronauts and Gravity

Because there is no gravity in space after an expedition the astronauts have to relearn how to walk and do normal activities again. Because they had been in an environment where there was no resistance, it actually proved to be detrimental to them. So they developed suits that would mirror the gravitational resistance to keep the astronauts familiar with normal resistance in pull. Resistance is necessary. **Tags: Problems, Persistence - Source: © Brian D. Hunter**

57. The Conditions Are Always Perfect

Until 2007 there had never been an NFL team who had won a Super Bowl whose home field had a domed stadium. The football teams who had a domed stadium were always used to playing in perfect conditions, so when they had to play in Buffalo in the snow facing freezing temperatures or the sweltering heat of Florida or Los Angeles, they struggled. God loves enough to make sure the conditions in our lives are not perfect. He knows if we are to be the best that we can be, we must have sunshine and rain. **Tags: Perspective - Source: © Brian D. Hunter**

58. The True Anointing

In Exodus 30 God gives the ingredients for the anointing oil that will be used in anointing ceremonies. He names Cassia, Calamus. Cinnamon, myrrh, and olive oil. What is interesting is that the anointing oil symbolic of the Holy Spirit was made up of bitter ingredients and sweet ingredients. You could not have the true anointing oil with just bitter ingredients, and you could not have it with just sweet ingredients. There must be a combination of both. To be truly anointed and empowered by the Spirit there will be some sweet times and some bitter times in our lives. We must have both. "I have learned in whatsoever state I am in to be content. I know how to be up and I know how to be down."
Tags: Growth, Holy Spirit - Source: © Brian D. Hunter

59. God Always Takes His Time

Listening to one of my favorite preachers, she made note of how God took his time to bring out certain gifts in her. She declared how God waited till she was in her thirties to call her to preach. He waited till she was in her forties to call her into the pastorate, and into her fifties for her to be an author. Never think that it is too late for God to do something in your life. God is not in a hurry and He will ultimately pull out what is inside of you.
Tags: Growth, Time - Source: Sheryl Brady

60. Sometimes It Takes Fertilizer

Though I am not fond of the smell of fertilizer, I am surprised by its purpose. Fertilizer is manure that is processed and used to grow plants. There are properties in the fertilizer that help the plants grow faster. Though none of us want to be in a mess, drama, chaos, or confusion, there are time when "mess" helps us to grow a little faster.   **Tags: Growth, Enemies - Source: © Brian D. Hunter**

61. The Codfish and Catfish

A number of years back the codfish industry on the northeast coast of the US had a problem. How could they keep the codfish fresh while they transported them across the country? When they froze the fish they lost too much flavor. When they transported them live in tanks filled with saltwater the fish got soft and mushy.

Finally they found a solution. They placed catfish in the tanks with the codfish. Catfish are a natural enemy of codfish, so the catfish would chase them around the tanks all the time they were being transported. The cod now arrived in better condition than ever because the constant motion helped them remain fresh. We all need catfish in our lives – the difficult people or situations in life that may not be pleasant but keep us healthy and growing. **Tags: Enemies - Source: Anonymous**

62. The Tower of Pisa

The La Torre Pisa, commonly known as the Leaning Tower of Pisa, has eight stories, and it leans forty-five degrees. It has been leaning for 840 years and has never fallen down. It has defied the laws of gravity and is still standing. You may be leaning but thank God you are still standing. **Tags: Perseverance - Source: © Brian D. Hunter**

63. Take Your Hands Off!

A parishioner came to her pastor because she didn't know how to forgive. He took her up to the bell tower, handed her the rope and asked her to ring the church bell. She rang it quite a few times and then he told her to let go of the rope. The bell rang for a few more minutes of its own accord and then it stopped. The pastor said, "That's how you forgive. As long as you have your hand on what the person did, you will be reminded of the offense. Forgiveness is taking your hand off of the offense. You may still feel the ring for a while but eventually it will stop."
Tags: Forgiveness - Source: Corrie Ten Boom

64. Listen to the Voice

After graduating high school, I had the opportunity to visit Germany. While there we visited a botanical garden. In the middle of the garden was a huge maze of hedges that were fifteen feet tall. We decided to walk through the maze. Some of my colleagues walked through it, easily finding the outlet. Once you had made it through, you could go up on a high platform and look down at others making their way through the maze. Navigating the maze was a little difficult for me and to make matters worse it was getting dark. I didn't want to be stuck in the maze alone. The only way I made it through the maze was by listening to the voice of the people above me, who could see the outlay of the maze and instructed me to the outlet. **Tags: Dependence, Faith - Source: © Brian D. Hunter**

65. Crushed Roses

One of my fondest childhood memories is spending time at my grandmother's house. Her house always smelled like fresh flowers. Every few days she would adorn her dining room table with flowers. When the flowers started to wilt I expected her to thrown them in the trash. But instead she would take the petals off the stem and crush them in a bowl and place them all over the house. Though they looked dead on the stem, as she crushed them they released a fragrance that still filled the room though they looked like they were dead. We may feel/look like it's all over, but God has a way of crushing us to the degree where there is still something left. **Tags: Value**

66. Squeeze the Toothpaste

My mother taught me a valuable lesson regarding a tube of toothpaste. I was going to discard a tube of toothpaste, my mother stopped me and asked why was I throwing toothpaste away? I said, "There is no more in there." She said, "Yes there is." She took the toothpaste and began rolling and squeezing the tube from the bottom and, lo and behold, there was a whole lot more toothpaste in there. Just when you think that it's all over God can squeeze more out of you and the situation. **Tags: Perseverance - Source: © Brian D. Hunter**

67. Cigarettes and the Word of God

Before there were laws in place, I remember as a little boy I could buy cigarettes. My aunt would send me to the local store with a note. All I did was give the note to the storekeeper and put the money on the counter. Without exchanging a word he would read the note, take the money, and hand me the cigarettes. Though the store keeper never saw my aunt, the authority was in the note she wrote and I simply read what was on the note. As a preacher I read the "note", the Bible, as God said it. It carries authority because He said it. **Tags: God's Word, Bible - Source: © Brian D. Hunter**

68. Stay Inside the Lines

All of my kids enjoyed coloring in coloring books. When they started they would use several different colors and they would never stay inside the lines. Though it was a hodgepodge mess I would still say how wonderful the picture was. As they "matured" they learned to use the proper colors and stay inside the lines, and I could see a vast improvement. Many of us know what it's like to be disobedient outside the lines, but as we mature we learn to stay in the lines as He has asked us to. **Tags: Maturity, Holiness - Source: © Brian D. Hunter**

69. Encourage Yourself

As my son began to learn how to walk, he would take a step or two and we would get so excited and clap for him. Every time he would take a step we would clap and make a big deal of it. I remember one time he took some steps and no one clapped for him. He paused for a moment waiting for the applause and when no one did, he just started clapping for himself.

Sometimes you can't wait for others to encourage you. Sometimes you have to encourage yourself. **Tags: Encouragement - Source: © Brian D. Hunter**

70. Encourage Mike Tyson!

I was an avid fan of the prizefighter Mike Tyson. He was hailed as a knockout artist. But I noticed as he was on his way to the ring there was a guy who was beside him the whole way, encouraging him. "You're the best, Mike." "Nobody like you, Mike." "You gonna get 'em tonight, Mike." But even when Mike Tyson lost, on his way from the ring the same guy was at his shoulder encouraging him. Whether we are up or down, winning or losing, we need someone to encourage us. **Tags: Encouragement - Source: © Brian D. Hunter**

71. Raise Your Arms Up!

I remember helping all of my kids when they were small to take their shirts off at the end of the day. When I would lift the shirt above their heads sometimes it got stuck. They couldn't see anything because the shirt was covering their face. As a result they began to struggle. I would admonish them to raise your arms! raise your arms! As long as they struggled and left their face and arms in the shirt they were confined. But as soon as they raised their arms I was able to lift the shirt right off. We struggle with things, and God is waiting for us to lift our arms in surrender to Him. When we surrender, He is able to take the burden away. **Tags: Freedom - Source: © Brian D. Hunter**

72. Bless the Lord

"Barak" is the Hebrew word for bless, which means to kneel. The word bless is a word that comes out of the culture of the times. As some travelers would go from place to place they traveled with camels who bore their wares. When they reached their destination they couldn't reach the top of the camel to get the stuff off his back. So they would take a stick and begin to hit the knees of the camel and yell "Barak! Barak!" The camel would eventually fall to its knees, thereby making it easy to get the burdens off his back. We too can have things that we are burdened down by. As long as we stand in our own pride and strength we will shoulder the burdens. But when we kneel in submission He is able to take the burdens off of us. **Tags: Burdens**

73. Alfred Hitchcock

Alfred Hitchcock is known as one of the best suspense directors in the business. But if you look closely, he makes cameo appearances in a number of his films. But you have to look close to really notice that he is in the picture. For example, in the "The Birds" he can be seen winding a clock. In "Dial M for Murder" he can be seen walking a dog. Though he was the director behind the scenes, he could also be seen in the middle of the action. Though God is the director, He can also be seen in the action of our lives, though sometimes we have to really look to see His face and hand in the action. **Tags: Providence**

74. Claude and Ray

One of my favorite movies is a comedy entitled "Life". "Life" is the story about two friends, Claude and Ray. They were framed for a crime that they didn't commit and sentenced to life in prison. Time and time again they plot several failed escape attempts, until one day Claude sets the infirmary on fire and runs into it as if he is trying to save Ray. The last time we see Claude and Ray they are in the fire headed to their deaths. But in the very next scene we see them in Yankee Stadium with their hands lifted and cheering. **Tags: Praise, Perseverance - Source: "Life" (1999), Universal Pictures**

75. I'm Under Pressure

Oftentimes we think that pressure is negative. However, the tires on a car must have pressure. Without pressure they would be flat and would not be able to take the car where it should go. Some of our pressure is good as it allows us to go from one place to the other. **Tags: Problems, Burdens - Source: © Brian D. Hunter**

76. I Can Call My Sister's Name

Growing up I was never one to like to fight. However, my sister never ran from a fight. She had a reputation in our neighborhood and as a result no one really messed with her. I remember going to the corner store, buying a big bag of candy. On the way back I was confronted by the neighborhood bully who was trying to snatch my bag of candy. I was panicked and afraid. Tears began to swell in my eyes. It was then that I had a bright idea. I just began to yell my sister's name. Though he couldn't see her, he knew of her reputation. I knew she wasn't home but he didn't. I kept calling her name and finally he ran off. There is a name that is above every name! The name of the Lord is a strong tower. **Tags: Dependence, Trust - Source: © Brian D. Hunter**

77. Keep On Pumping

There is an old story about a world famous organist. To play the organ, air had to be pumped into the organ as he pressed the keys. The famous organist played the first half of a concert to a thunderous applause. The famous organist went backstage and said to the man who was responsible for pumping air into the organ, "Man, those people sure do love me!" His assistant said, "Don't you mean they loved us?" The organist responded, "No, those people are clapping for me. I just played a masterpiece." His assistant didn't argue with him. As the organist went for the next set of the concert, hee sat at the bench and put his fingers on the keys. When he pressed them, nothing came out. He

pressed again and still nothing happened. The people who were cheering were now laughing and jeering. He said to his assistant, "Man, we got a show to do, start pumping the air!" to which the assistant replied, "Well you did so well the first time without me, I just thought that you would do it again."
We never succeed by ourselves. We always need the help of someone else. **Tags: Dependence, Friendship - Source: Anonymous**

78. Broadway Dancer

There was an aspiring dancer whose sole dream was to dance on Broadway. She practiced for hours upon hours, hoping that someday she would grace the stage. One day her friends got together and discouraged her so badly that not only did she give up dancing, but she also decided to commit suicide. So she went to the Golden Gate Bridge and before she jumped off she began to write a suicide note that began by saying "They said . . ." After writing it she jumped to her death. When the police got there all they found was a note that read "They said . . ." The morning headline for the *San Francisco Chronicle* read "Young aspiring dancer jumps to her death; cause unknown, but something they said made her do it." Sometimes you can't listen to what they say. **Tags: Encouragement, Persistence - Source: Anonymous**

79. Duck Forgiveness

An old story is told of a little boy who loved to throw rocks in the yard. Time and time again he was told by his mother, "Son, don't throw rocks." Despite her admonition he continued to throw rocks. One day he threw a rock and hit and killed his mother's prized duck. He thought no one saw him until dinner time was over and his sister said, "If you don't do the dishes for me, I am gonna tell mother about the duck." For an entire week his sister made him do chores and if he refused she would say, "Remember the duck?" After two long weeks of being enslaved by his sister who was holding the mistake over his head, he

couldn't take it anymore. He ran to his mother and confessed that he had killed the duck. After his tearful confession his mother said, "Son, I saw you when you did it. I was just waiting for you to come and tell me you did it so I could forgive you."
Tags: Forgiveness - Source: Anonymous

80. Barry's Mercedes

I had a friend in high school who loved Mercedes Benz cars. Every day he would wear a Mercedes Benz hat. We would ridicule him from time to time because he wore a Mercedes hat but didn't own a Mercedes. Later he not only donned the hat but he also secured a key chain, and we continued to ridicule him. After graduation, still in our caps and gowns, we looked in disbelief as Barry sat in a brand new Mercedes Benz. Unbeknownst to us Barry was told by his father that if he achieved a certain GPA upon graduation he would buy him a Mercedes Benz. Though he didn't have the car yet, he was already acting like it. So when he got the car the hat and the key chain were already in place. **Tags: Encouragement, Perseverance - Source: © Brian D. Hunter**

81. My Father Sees a Winner in Me

In high school I was the 400 meter league champion two years in row. I have competed overseas in places such as Germany and Holland. However, my track and field career didn't start so well. In sixth and seventh grade, I literally lost every race. After the race, my dad would say, "Don't worry about it, there is a winner in you." That sounded ridiculous to me because surely he had seen that I had just lost the race, and yet he had the audacity to say I was a winner? But from eighth grade to my senior year in high school I never lost a race. After my last race as a senior, my dad reminded me that he had known there was a winner in me. Though I couldn't see it, he always could see the best in me. **Tags: Maturity, Growth - Source: © Brian D. Hunter**

82. The Creator is Back

Upon reading the biography of Steve Jobs it was interesting to note that though he was one of the founders of the Apple, he was fired from his own company. Steve Jobs was the innovator and creator of several Apple products. Once they let him go they discovered that profits and innovations were at an all time low. They decided to ask him back, and almost overnight profits began to soar because they had the creator back in his place.
Tags: Dependence

83. Britney Spears

Many of us witnessed the meteoric rise to fame of Britney Spears. We also witnessed how her life began to spiral out of control based on that same success. Her life was out of control, and it seemed like no one could get to her.
That is until her father stepped onto the scene. Her father actually moved in with her, went where she went, and took control of her affairs. After her father moved in her life began to change for the better.   **Tags: Dependence - Source: © Brian D. Hunter**

84. Emmitt Smith and Y.A.C.

One night while watching Monday night football, the legendary coach and commentator John Madden witnessed the running back expertise of Emmitt Smith.
Upon witnessing Smith's prowess, he actually invented a new statistical category for him. John Madden invented a category called "YAC", which stands for "yards after contact". Emmitt Smith was not only known for how many yards he achieved but also how many yards he was able to achieve after being hit.
Tags: Perseverance - Source: John Madden

85. Preparing for the Fight

A moose spends a great deal of time eating in the summer, for he knows in the fall there is a mating battle. The strongest bucks get to mate. So the moose knows in order to get ready for the battle in the fall, he must prepare in the summer. He can't get ready for the battle in the fall, he must be prepared beforehand. We can't wait for the enemy to attack and then prepare. We must prepare beforehand. **Tags: Preparation, Temptation - Source: Anonymous**

86. Friends Helping Friends

My son participated in his first track meet when he was five years of age. Being a former track and field star, I gave him as many pointers as I could. He was slated to run the 50 yard dash. I was proud to watch him win his race. After his race, in the next heat, I witnessed something I had never seen in track and field history. Two little girls were running side by side, matching each other stride for stride. Then all of a sudden one of the girls tripped and fell. The rest of the runners kept going towards the finish line. The girl who is running next to the girl who fell stopped and went back to help the girl get up. They ran to the finish line together. **Tags: Friendship - Source: © Brian D. Hunter**

87. Wisdom of Ants

Ants can carry one hundred times their body weight. An ant was carrying a piece of straw. He approached a large gap in the sidewalk, and after circling for a while he did something genius. He took the piece of straw out of his mouth and laid it across the gap and walked over it. Once he was on the other side he picked up the straw and continued to move on. **Tags: Burdens, Strength, Perseverance - Source: Anonymous**

88. Lesson from WD-40

Growing up I was very familiar with a product called WD-40. The blue and yellow WD-40 can has a variety of uses, but most often we used it to quiet squeaky door hinges. Though I had used the WD-40 I didn't know what it meant. I discovered WD-40 means "Water Displacement 40th Attempt." It took the scientists 39 times before they perfected it. On the 40th try it was perfected. Never give up! You are one try away from success. **Tags: Perseverance - Source: © Brian D. Hunter**

89. Giving and Receiving

There are two bodies of water in the middle east; the Dead Sea and the Sea of Galilee. The Sea of Galilee is teaming and thriving with life. The Dead Sea on the other hand is lifeless and nothing thrives or survives there. The difference is the Dead Sea only takes in water and never releases it. As a result it is stagnant and lifeless. But the Sea of Galilee not only takes in water but it also releases water as well. So there is a constant receiving and releasing. **Tags: Giving, Money - Source: © Brian D. Hunter**

90. Dressed for the Occasion

While in the airport leaving Palm Springs, California to go back to Oakland, California, I noticed a gentleman that, though we were in over 100 degree heat, was wearing a coat and scarf. I couldn't resist asking him why he was wearing a coat and scarf in Palm Springs. He replied, "I am on my way to Northern California and it is very cold there so I am just dressed for where I am going." **Tags: Perspective, Trust - Source: © Brian D. Hunter**

91. Which Side of the Window?

I recall taking a flight recently and noticed that on my side of the plane it was completely dark, yet on the other side of the plane was bright sunshine. Same plane, but different points of view. Life's perspective can depend on what side of the "plane" you are looking out of.   **Tags: Perspective - Source: © Brian D. Hunter**

92. Cool and Comfortable

While a student at Biola University, I was commissioned to do an outreach project in southern California on one of the hottest days that summer. I looked around campus for my friend who would be helping me in this endeavor. I searched the campus and couldn't find him anywhere. I finally got word that he was in the chapel. When I walked into the chapel I approached cautiously just in case he was praying or meditating. Instead of sitting he was laying down on the pew, asleep. I asked why he was there and his response was it was the only place on campus where the air conditioner was working. So he was not there to communion with God or to practice any of the spiritual disciplines but rather to be cool and comfortable. **Tags: Complacency - Source: © Brian D. Hunter**

93. Clap On, Clap Off

I was intrigued by a product that took the gadget world by storm. It was called a "Clapper". The Clapper changed how we turn off a light. Wherever you were in the room all you had to do was clap and the light would shut off. Clap again and it would come back on. The power of on and off was determined by a clap. Our praise can shut some things down and start other things. **Tags: Praise - Source: © Brian D. Hunter**

94. How Heavy Is It?

How heavy does something have to be, to be too heavy? Consider the following story: A psychologist walked around a room while teaching stress management to an audience. As she raised a glass of water, everyone expected they'd be asked the "half empty or half full" question. Instead, with a smile on her face, she enquired, "How heavy is this glass of water?" Answers called out ranged from eight to twenty ounces. She replied, "The absolute weight doesn't matter. It depends on how long I hold it. If I hold it for a minute, it's not a problem. If I hold it for an hour, I'll have an ache in my arm. If I hold it for a day, my arm will feel numb and paralyzed. In each case, the weight of the glass doesn't change, but the longer I hold it, the heavier it becomes." **Tags: Burdens, Release - Source: Anonymous**

95. James Brown

James Brown shares in his autobiography that he was born dead. We would call it still born today. After several attempts to hit him on the bottom to stir up a response nothing happened. His aunt Minnie pushed everyone aside and put her mouth on his mouth and breathed into his lungs to help give him oxygen until he began to take his own first breaths. Sometimes when life has gotten the best of us we need someone to breath new life into us. **Tags: Friendship**

96. Let Everything That Has Breath

The Psalmist declares, "Let everything that has breath praise the Lord." Every time we take a breath, several things begin to happen. Our breathing is actually a defense mechanism that keeps things out of our system that could hurt or kill us. Breathing blocks out germs and bacteria that could penetrate and ultimately kill us. When you breathe the hairs in your nose block out and filter germs. The trachea is moist and catches germs and bacteria. The lungs have tiny cilia hairs moving back and forth to keep things out of our lungs, preventing pneumonia from setting in. All this is done in the quick seconds we take a breath. It blocks and prevents. So when we praise and use our breath it is literally blocking things that could hurt and discourage us. **Tags: Praise - Source: © Brian D. Hunter**

97. Uncle Earl's Polaroid Camera

I have fond memories of our family gathering for holidays and special occasions. Though there was always someone taking pictures, on this occasion my uncle was taking pictures with a camera I had never seen before. The camera was square with an accordion like lens. When he took a picture, he pulled the actual picture out from the side of the camera. When he pulled it out there was no picture on it yet. He began to shake the picture vigorously. As he shook it the picture began to develop in his hand. The more he shook, the more the picture developed. What was gray and dreary was now a bright and beautiful picture. But the beautiful picture could not have been developed without the shaking. **Tags: Maturity, Development - Source: © Brian D. Hunter**

98. Changing a Tire

One of the rites of passage for Hunter men is learning how to change a tire. My father's father taught him, my father taught me, and I have now taught my son. Though my son was taught to change a tire when the tire wasn't flat. The day came when it wasn't a drill; we actually had a flat tire. My son jumped out the car to change the tire because he knew what to do! Though he had watched and was instructed, he had never really lifted the tire or taken off the lug nuts. As he tried to do certain things, he knew it was beyond his physical strength. So as he watched and assisted, I changed the tire. When we got back in the car, his sister asked him, "What did you do?" He said, "I know how to change the tire myself. But because daddy was out there I just handed him what he needed and let him handle the heavy stuff." **Tags: Dependence, Burdens - Source: © Brian D. Hunter**

99. Take Your Burdens to the Lord

After every Sunday morning service, the pastor noticed that where a certain parishioner sat there were several pieces of balled up paper. One day the pastor asked why he continued to leave trash in the sanctuary. He responded, "Pastor, that is not trash, but rather prayer requests. Throughout the course of the service I am writing prayer requests. You taught us to take our burdens to the Lord and leave them there. So I leave my prayer requests here in the sanctuary trusting that God will answer and I don't leave burdened by them." **Tags: Prayer, Burdens - Source: Anonymous**

100. It Comes Out in the Wash

Every now and then I noticed after washing clothes that there is change left in the drum of the washing machine. The change left in the drum of the washing machine has fallen out of pockets in the wash. As the wash goes through its cycle, change falls out based on the "agitator" shaking it loose. The pockets held monetary value, but the value was only revealed after being agitated in the wash. There are times when our greatest value is revealed as we are being "agitated." **Tags: Afflictions, Value - Source: © Brian D. Hunter**

101. What an Opportunity

Now the Chinese do not have letters in their alphabet like we do. Rather, the Chinese use characters and symbols for their alphabet. Their symbol for 'crisis' actually combines two symbols: danger and opportunity. So when they see crisis there is the presentation of danger but there is also the possibility of opportunity. When there is a crisis it is a prime opportunity for God to show himself strong in your crisis. **Tags: Dependence**

102. Ship Rocking

One summer, while hosting family from the east coast, we took a boat ride on the San Francisco Bay. While we were sailing, a couple of people got sea sick. I tried to help them, but to no avail. Luckily the captain of our vessel knew something about sailing that a lot of folks on the boat did not. When you are sailing and encounter waves that are rocking the boat up and down, to and fro, you have to find something that is steady and keep your eyes on it.

In your times of storm, you have to keep your eye on Jesus, who is steady, so that when everything else is up and down and bouncing around, you can maintain your stability.

Tags: Perspective - Source: © Brian D. Hunter

103. The Power Source

I remember visiting a family member in the hospital. Upon making my way to the room, I saw a gentleman walking very slowly with an IV connected to his arm. He started walking around the corridors of the hallways very slowly. He passed me again, walking a little faster. And after a few minutes he passed me again walking even faster. As I exited I told him I saw him moving slowly at first when he was connected and then faster and faster. Why was that? His reply was, "Before I was hooked up to the IV I had little strength. But because I remained connected to the IV I am gaining strength to walk every minute." Even in times where we seem to have no strength, as long as we stay connected to the Holy Spirit, He will gives us strength for the journey. **Tags: Strength - Source: © Brian D. Hunter**

104. Rebounds and Second Chances

When I was a teenager I was a big fan of the Chicago Bulls. They had arguably the best player of all time, Michael Jordan. He also had the best side kick in all of sports history, Scottie Pippen. If one of them couldn't score, they would dish the ball out to the three point line to either Craig Hodges, B.J.

Armstrong, or Steve Kerr. They were bad! I cheered for Mike, Scottie, Craig, B.J., and Steve because they made it look so easy winning six championships. But I learned that in several of their seasons, their success wasn't because of their offense. Mike missed some shots! Scottie missed some shots. Craig, B.J., and Steve all missed their fair share of shots! But they had another player; he was pretty weird by most standards. He had piercings. His body was covered in tattoos. His name was Dennis Rodman! And his job was to get rebounds. When Mike or somebody else missed, Dennis got the rebound and gave the Bulls a second chance!

The only reason I have any success in life is because of Jesus Christ. Jesus went to Calvary for us, claimed the ultimate victory, and through him God gave us a second chance so that we can now be victorious! **Tags: Redemption, Salvation Source: © Brian D. Hunter**

105. Dusty the Car Chaser

A friend of mine rescued Dusty from the pound. Dusty is trusted companion. But, Diva had some issues. Dusty liked to chase cars. He'd be out there chasing cars and they would say, "Dusty, don't do it!" but he still chased cars. They paid good money for obedience school. But as soon as he got outside, he was chasing cars. He refused to stop. One evening, they heard the sound of screeching tires and a crying dog. There was Dusty. He had been hit by a car, and he was dragging his bruised and bloody body. They rushed him to the veterinarian. The vet explained that Dusty has serious injuries which would require surgery. You have two choices. For $7,000.00 and we can save him. Or, pay us $15.00 and we can put him to sleep. They prayed right there in the vet's office. They decided to pay the $7,000. We, too, were like Diva. We were doing some things that we know we ought not to have done, and we got caught up in sin over and over again. We were bloody and bruised, and yet we dragged ourselves God's house. And God said, I have a choice. I can give my Son on Calvary, or let you die. I'm so glad that Jesus paid the high price on Calvary. **Tags: Redemption, Salvation Source: © Brian D. Hunter**

Illustration Index
(Illustrations Tags)

The illustration tags are in alphabetical order. The numbers do not refer to page numbers but to the illustration numbers.

Afflictions - 100

Bible - 67

Burdens - 25, 54, 72, 74, 87, 94, 98, 99

Change - 42

Complacency - 92

Deliverance - 49

Dependence - 50, 64, 76, 77, 82, 83, 98, 101

Development - 97

Encouragement - 70, 78, 80

Endurance - 3, 8, 17, 18, 22, 23

Enemies - 2, 43, 45, 60, 61

Faith - 7, 20, 21, 27, 64

LIFE HAPPENS

BUT GOD

ORCHESTRATES

Illustrations That Connect

90 DAY

DEVOTIONAL

Use Your S.O.A.P.

S.O.A.P. stands for Scripture, Observation, Application and Prayer. It is a way of getting more out of your time in God's word.

How does it work?

It's quite simple. As you read the following daily devotionals, read the bible verse as you normally would with one simple difference. In a journal make note of any verses that jump out at you with special significance. This is the basis for diving deeper and using S.O.A.P.

- **Scripture**
Write down what stuck out to you in your reading.

- **Observation**
What did you observe about the scripture that struck you. This can be one sentence or a whole book.

- **Application**
How can you apply the observation so that it affects your life today.

- **Prayer**
Write out a prayer to God based on what you just learned and ask him to help you apply this truth in your life.

DAY 1

....See I have set before you an open door

and no man can shut it . . .

Rev. 3:8

One of my all-time favorite retail stores is Walmart. I love the prices and deals in Walmart. Real Walmart shoppers go in for one item and come out with a cart full of items.

I remember taking a trip to Walmart with my daughter, and in her youthful excitement she ran ahead of me to the entrance. Much to her dismay as she stood in front of the door, the door did not swing open as usual.
She looked back and said, "Daddy, I think Walmart is closed! I am standing at the door and it is not opening." I said, "Oh? Well, let's stand there together and see what happens."

I grabbed her hand and we stood on the entrance mat together, and the door flung wide open. Puzzled, she asked, "Why didn't it open when I stood there by myself?" I replied, "You don't have enough weight and influence for the door to open. But when you stand there with daddy, I have more weight and influence than you do, and I can cause doors to open that would never open for you."

DAY 2

But I say unto Love your enemies, bless those that curse you do good to those that hate you, and pray for those which despitefully use you, and persecute you

Matt. 5:44

The late Dr. Howard Thurman tells the story of his grandmother, who lived next door to a lady who did not care for her at all.

To prove her disdain for his grandmother, she would shovel chicken manure over the fence.

Her neighbor fell sick, and Dr. Thurman's grandmother went to the hospital to visit her, carrying a bouquet of flowers in her hand. As she walked in, her neighbor was shocked and surprised. "Why are you here? And where did you get those flowers? I know you can't afford flowers as beautiful as those." She replied, "Well, these flowers are really from you. Remember everyday you would shovel chicken manure in my yard in anger and spitefulness. When in fact all you were doing was fertilizing these fresh flowers."

DAY 3

But those that wait upon the Lord shall renew strength;
they shall mount up with wings like eagles; they shall run
and not be weary; they shall walk and not faint.

Isaiah 40:31

I have never professed to have green thumb, but I have tried my hand at gardening. I planted flowers in my flowerbed known as perennials. Perennials possess very bright colors such as yellow and purple. I was proud of the colors that illuminated my yard.

One day to my shock and dismay, I came home and the flowers that once were so beautiful were now wilted and brown. Once, they had punctuated my yard with vibrant colors, but now they were about to be uprooted and discarded. But just in the nick of time, my neighbor informed me that these were perennials. Underneath the soil they have a bulb. They go through a life cycle where during the colder months they "die" and it looks like they are wilted and dead. But don't count them out; leave them in the soil. When the season changes they will come back to life in full bloom, once again displaying their beautiful colors

DAY 4

I will bless the Lord at all times
his praise shall continually be in mouth

Psalm 34:1

I enjoy listening to music as I drive. Though I don't possess the gift to sing, I love to sing along with the music in the car.

Every now and then I would hit a hard bump in the road and the CD would stop but I continued to sing. A few seconds later the music would come back on. Though I encountered a bump on the road, I never stopped singing.

As we navigate down the road of life, it's easy to keep a praise on our lips when everything is going smooth. Ultimately we will all encounter some bumps in the road. Don't let the bumps in the road stop your praise.

DAY 5

I have been young and now am old;
yet I have not seen the righteous forsaken nor his
descendants begging bread
Psalm 37:25

One of the life lessons my father taught me was to always get a receipt after a purchase. The receipt was proof that a particular price had been paid for a particular item.

To the casual observer they see your progress, praise, happiness, and joy. When others see the way you worship and serve, they may have no idea the price you had to pay. They have no idea all the things that you have had to go through just to be who you are.

So we ought to think twice when we are jealous and envious of others. You never know the price that was paid.

DAY 6

*O magnify the LORD with me
and let us exalt his name together*

Psalm 34:3

I love to ride roller coasters! I love the surprise and exhilaration of every twist, drop, and turn.

The true sign of a real, seasoned roller coaster rider is that you are screaming at the top of your voice and you keep your arms up the whole ride. Through every up and down, through every twist and turn, a real roller coaster rider keeps their voice lifted and hands up.

As life takes you through ups and downs, through twists and turns, we need to keep our voices lifted and hands up in praise.

DAY 7

Now faith is the substance of things hoped for and the evidence of things not seen
Hebrews 11:1

Under the Obama administration, the navy seals caught and killed one of the world's most wanted men: Osama bin Laden.

Though we never saw a corpse as evidence that he was dead, we still believed it, based on the word we were given.

There are times we have to believe simply based on God's Word. Though we have not seen any tangible evidence we must hold on to His word and promise. As you go through this day, though there may be little to no evidence of God's hand moving on your behalf. Stand on His word!

DAY 8

. . . For I have learned in whatever state

I am to be content

Philippians 4:11

One of my favorite prizefighters was "'Iron" Mike Tyson. He was known as a knockout artist, knocking out his opponents in the first few minutes of the fight. Though he held the title as the Heavyweight Champion, we really didn't know what he was made of until the tables were turned; when he began taking some hard punches, and was knocked down.

We began to see just who he really was. He began fighting dirty, hitting below the belt, and of course the infamous incident where he bit off the top of his opponent's ear. Only after being knocked down did we see the man he really was.

Being on "top" doesn't always reveal who we really are. It's only after taking some "punches" and even getting knocked down by life's circumstances that we are able to see who we really are. What is really on the inside often surfaces in times of hardship.

DAY 9

That I may know him in the power of his resurrection

Philippians 3:10

There is an old story told of a Sunday School promotion exercise where all the graduates were asked to recite the 23rd Psalm from memory.

First up was a seven-year-old boy, and he began reciting the Psalm. He did it with no mistakes, fluid and articulate. Everyone was so proud of him.

After he was finished, an elderly woman made her way slowly to the podium, and she began reciting the 23rd Psalm. As she began to recite it, the congregation became silent, hanging on to her every word. Tears began to flow from faces in the congregation as she spoke with power and conviction.

Though they both quoted the same Psalm, the difference was the little boy knew the 23rd Psalm, but the elderly lady knew the Shepherd that was in the 23rd Psalm through years of experience with the Shepherd. Do you really know the Good Shepherd? Or just about the Good Shepherd?

DAY 10

. . . You thought evil against me
but God meant it unto my good . . .

Genesis 50:20

One of my all-time favorite Christmas gifts was a Kodak camera. I loved the state of the art, sleek rectangular design. I took great care of the camera, making sure I bought only quality film. I enjoyed "snapping" the 24 exposures of film.

After I had exhausted all the exposures, I would drop off the film at Fotomat to be developed. In about three or four days the pictures would be ready for pick up. When I received the pictures back, they were in an envelope that had two compartments. The bright, colorful pictures were always in the front and the negatives were in the back. The negatives, though they are dark and you can't really make out what the picture is, are very necessary, as you cannot have the beautiful color pictures without the dark negatives. Furthermore, the negatives are always smaller and fewer than the actual pictures.

We see and cherish the bright pictures in our lives, but never forget that if it wasn't for the negatives in our lives they could never produce the bright pictures. Remember our negatives are always smaller than the beautiful picture that God is developing in us.

DAY 11

The entrance of thy word brings light
and gives understanding to the simple

Psalm 119:130

Mathematics has never been one of my strengths. I struggled through most math classes in school. When my fifth grade teacher would assign homework there were always two groups of students: one group would be assigned the even numbered problems, and the other group the odd numbered problems.

I was always in the odd numbered group, and I would struggle for what seemed like hours with my math homework. I had a friend who shared the same difficulties as I did with math, but for some strange reason he would always get all the problems correct. I was baffled. He was no smarter than I was, but he aced the homework.

He shared a secret with me. He said, "The teacher knows we have trouble with the problems, but still wants us to succeed and build confidence in our math skills. So all the answers to the odd numbered problems are in the back of the book. If you are having trouble with a problem, you don't have to struggle, just look in the back of the book and the answer is there."

The Lord knows we will encounter problems and will be looking for answers. Instead of becoming overwhelmed and frustrated we ought to look in the Book to find the answers. The answers to our problem is already in the there.

DAY 12

I can do all things through Christ
which strengthens me
Philippians 4:13

Early on I was keenly aware of what my academic strengths were. Needless to say math was not one of them. My father would spend hours trying to help me understand math. One night we wrestled with long division for hours and for the life of me I couldn't grasp it. It started getting late, so my dad actually ended up working out the problems for me.

When I got to school the next day my teacher was shocked that I had every problem correct. So of course she wanted me to come up to the board and show the class how I got the answers. I was sweating and nervous because I didn't know how to do it, all I knew is that my father worked out the problem. I had to admit to her and the entire class that I didn't solve the problems myself, but my daddy actually solved every problem. I said, "I am just presenting to you what he did, though I can't explain what he did."

When the problem is too complex, our heavenly Father takes over and develops answers on our behalf. Even when we try to explain how He did it, it is impossible, all we know is "Daddy" did all the work.

DAY 13

You will keep him in perfect peace
whose mind is stayed on you
Isaiah 26:3

I am an animal lover, at least from afar. However, one of my childhood friends loved animals up close and personal. He tracked down and captured a lizard in his hand and was showing it off.

Unfortunately, he lost control of the lizard and in his attempt to recapture it he made a colossal mistake. He grabbed the lizard by its tail and much to his surprise, the lizard's tail broke loose, and the lizard continued to run for its freedom.

The lizard lost its tail but didn't lose its head. Though he may have lost a portion of his tail, the lizard never turned around to see what happened or complain. The lizard understood the portion of his tail that he lost would eventually grow back.

Though we may lose some things from time to time (money, time, relationships, opportunity, etc.), we must remember never to lose our head. As long as we don't lose our head, all that was lost can be recovered. As long as we don't lose our head we can THINK of the goodness of God and how time and time again He can recover what is lost.

DAY 14

Do nothing out of selfish ambition or vain conceit, but in humility value others above yourself

Philippians 2:3

Most professional football lineman are tall, big men. However the key to their success is not necessarily their height or strength, but how low they can get as they execute a hit. The lower a lineman gets, the easier it is to knock down his opponent.

Our success is not always found in our arrogance , pride, and strength, but in how low and how humble we can be by depending of God.

ARE YOU USING YOUR S.O.A.P. ?

- **Scripture**

Write down what stuck out to you in your reading.

- **Observation**

What did you observe about the scripture that struck you. This can be one sentence or a whole book.

- **Application**

How can you apply the observation so that it affects your life today.

- **Prayer**

Write out a prayer to God based on what you just learned and ask him to help you apply this truth in your life.

Day 15

*Humble yourself under the mighty hand
of God and in due time he will exalt you
in due time*

1 Peter 5:6-7

As a pastor, I constantly use my voice. I was told that hot tea, lemon, and honey were good for the throat. Being a purveyor of fine tea, I have discovered there are different kinds of tea drinkers.

There are some people who are "dippers" and others who are "remainers". Dippers hold the tea bag in the hot water for a little bit and then take it out. They dip again and take it out. A constant in and out. Employing this method, the tea bag never releases its full favor.

On the other end of the spectrum there are those who plunge the tea bag one time and leave it submerged in the hot water. As a result the full flavor is released. The tea bag changes the color and environment of the cup.

Which will you be? One who is in and out of the "hot water" or one who will remain faithful even under hostile and adverse conditions?

DAY 16

God is our refuge and strength
a very present help in time of trouble
Psalm 46:1

My daughter and I were watching a documentary about police officers on patrol. In distress, a lady called 911 emergency dispatch. She reached the dispatcher, but she was in so much distress, all she could do was scream and cry. She never stated the problem, she never gave her name, and she never gave her address. But within minutes the police were knocking at her door.

My daughter was stunned and amazed. She asked, "How did the police know where she lived if she never told them?" I explained to her that anytime someone calls 911, the telephone number and the address are displayed on the dispatcher's screen so they know exactly where a person is even if they can't say it.

If the police dispatcher can locate and help without knowing where the lady lived or what her problem was. Then how much more is our God able to locate and help us even though we may not be able to articulate the problem?

DAY 17

Confess your faults one to another and pray for one another
James 5:16

During our summer vacations, my sister and I would explore the hotel we were staying in. We would locate the pool, sauna, weight room, etc. Of course we would play on the elevator. On one of our infamous elevator rides I decided to push all the buttons at the same time and as a result the elevator became stuck. I panicked and began pushing buttons, ringing the alarm but to no avail, the elevator was not moving.

I was in a panic but my sister remained calm. She pointed out that there was a small door on the inside panel of the elevator. She opened up the panel and picked up a red phone which was located inside. The line was answered right away. My sister told the man on the line that the elevator had stopped and we were stuck inside. In a matter of seconds, the elevator jerked once and began making its way to the next floor.

The elevator was stuck, preventing us from going to the next level. I didn't voice the concern myself, however my sister acted as my intercessor by calling up the man who could fix the problem and take us to another level.

DAY 18

We are troubled on every side, yet not distressed;
we are perplexed, but not in despair, Persecuted, but not forsaken;
cast down, but not destroyed
2 Corinthians 4:8-9

One the greatest sensations of the 70s was a toy called a Weeble. I enjoyed singing the tagline "Weebles wobble but they won't fall down." You could hit it, punch it, slam it down on the ground, but regardless of how it was treated, a Weeble always bounced back up.

Later I discovered that each Weeble had a small weight on the bottom so that when knocked down the weight would help them bounce right back up.

We may be knocked down from time to time by the circumstances of life, but we are able to bounce back because we have the Holy Ghost on the inside that allows us to bounce back each and every time.

DAY 19

God resists the proud
but gives grace to the humble
James 4:6

A group of mountain climbers set out to conquer a mountain. Among their ranks was a novice who was embarking on his first climb. For several hours they climbed. At last they reached the plateau they had set their sights on. Once they got to the top of the mountain the first time climber stood straight up with arms raised and yelled, "I did it"!

As he celebrated his climbing accomplishment a strong gust of wind almost blew him off the mountaintop. The more experienced climbers explained to him that when you get to the top of a mountain you never stand straight up, but rather you drop to your knees to avoid being blown off the mountaintop. We should remember after climbing and reaching certain levels of success.

We should never gloat in our own success, but rather be humbled knowing that we could have never have made it without God's help.

DAY 20

*But God hath chosen the foolish things of the world
to confound the wise; and God hath chosen the weak things of the
world to confound the things which are mighty*
1 Corinthians 1:27

A little boy was standing in the middle of a city block for quite some time. An elderly man had been watching him and asked him, "What are you waiting for?" The boy answered, "I am waiting for the bus." The elderly gentleman said, "Well if you want to catch a bus, you have to wait at a bus stop. Buses only stop at bus stops."

The little boy replied, "No, I am going to catch the bus right here." The elderly gentlemen retorted, "But son, a bus will not stop here. They only stop at designated bus stops." The little boy replied again, "No, I am going to continue waiting right here."

So the elderly gentleman gave up and began to walk away. All of a sudden he heard the screeching of bus tires. As the little boy stepped onto the bus he looked back over his shoulder and said, "My daddy is the bus driver and he will stop wherever I am standing."

It may not make sense to others what God has instructed us to do, but our obedience will yield some great rewards.

DAY 21

Not only so, but we also glory in our sufferings, because we know that suffering produces perseverance; perseverance, character; and character, hope

Romans 5:3-5

A little boy had the pleasure of witnessing a butterfly attempting to break out of its cocoon. He noticed that the butterfly was really struggling to get out of the cocoon.

So he had a bright idea, and decided to help the butterfly get free. He began to break and peel off the cocoon in an effort to end the butterfly's struggle. With the boy's help, when the butterfly was free from the cocoon, instead of flying to heights unknown he fell to the ground and eventually died.

He failed to realize that as the butterfly struggles to get out of his cocoon, the butterfly is developing the strength and the ability to fly. The struggle is necessary.

DAY 22

For we are his workmanship, created in Christ Jesus unto good works,
which God hath before ordained that we should walk in them.
Ephesians 2:10

I own a couple of shirts that have my initials monogrammed on the cuff. Though I normally have them dry cleaned, every now and then I have to wash and iron them. To get the wrinkles out I must apply heat and pressure.

I had to make sure as I went out in public that all the wrinkles were out and it was presentable. Since my name was on the shirt, the condition and the way it looked was a reflection of me. So I worked hard to get all the wrinkles out.

God will spend time getting the "wrinkles" out of our life because we are reflections of Him. His name is on our lives, so we must submit to the "smoothing out" process, which may involve heat and pressure.

DAY 23

It is good for me that I have been afflicted;
that I might learn thy statutes.
Psalm 119:71

During an interesting animal documentary, I learned when a baby giraffe is born in the wild it immediately stands on its feet. Shockingly, the mother giraffe takes her long, strong neck and knocks the baby giraffe back down to the ground. The baby giraffe gets back up to its feet again, and again the mother knocks him down. With dogged determination and on wobbly legs, the baby giraffe gets back up again.

In disbelief, again I witnessed the mother giraffe knock the baby giraffe down. After several knock downs, the baby giraffe was able to stand sturdy and run with the rest of the herd. The mother giraffe's actions may be shocking but the mother knows there are predators who are waiting to devour her baby. Their legs need to be as strong and sturdy as possible to keep up with the herd. So every time the baby giraffe got knocked down, it strengthened him for the journey ahead.

God allows us to be knocked down, but it is really for our good. It increases our stamina and strength to prepare for the enemy and give us strength for the journey.

DAY 24

All that the Father gives Me will come to Me, and the one who comes to Me I will certainly not cast out.

John 6:37

I had to make a return at one of my favorite department stores. I had my original receipt and the original packaging with all the parts in the box. In front of me was a lady who had a doll that was not in its package. The doll's arm was hanging off; it was clearly used and damaged. I thought to myself, *They will never take that back in such terrible condition.*

But much to my surprise they took the doll back in spite of the condition that it was in. That day I discovered something about Walmart's return policy. They took the doll back regardless of its condition because they affix a sticker on the product to remind them that the product is theirs, and no matter what the condition they will always take it back.

We serve a God who takes us back despite the condition. His name is connected to us, and because we are connected to him He is able to restore whatever the condition may be.

DAY 25

Come unto me all you who labor and I will give you rest
Matthew 11:28

I was studying at my desk and needed a book from a shelf in another room. I asked my then four-year-old daughter to go get it for me. I described the color and size, and she was off to get it for me. I knew it was a big book, but I thought she could handle it.

As she was trying to bring it back to me I heard her straining and grunting under the weight and size of the book, yet she was trying her best to bring it to me. After hearing her struggle for a minute, I got up to help her.

Though she was struggling with the book, I didn't grab it out of her hand. I just picked her up while she still held the book in her hand and brought her back to my desk.

When our load is heavy and we are having a hard time managing, God may not take the load away but will strengthen and sustain us as we deal with it.

DAY 26

But the Comforter, [which is] the Holy Ghost, whom the Father will send in my name, he shall teach you all things, and bring all things to your remembrance, whatsoever I have said unto you.

John 14:26

Cell phones have changed the way we communicate. Though cell phones are considered advanced technology there is a major flaw; while talking on a cell phone, you may hear the background noise better than you can hear the person you are intending to talk to.

The background noise drowns out the intended voice. The enemy wants to ensure that God's voice is drowned out and the background noise of negativity and unbelief become louder than his voice. Can you hear Him now?

DAY 27

I wait for the LORD, my soul does wait and in his word do I hope

Psalm 130:5

My children love going to Target. One day, I promised them that we were going to stop by Target. After hearing the promise of a Target visit they began to sing as children do, "We are going to Target! We are going to Target!" over and over.

They had not made it to Target but they were already singing and celebrating the fact that they knew they were on the way.

Though we have not arrived at the place God has promised or received what we have been waiting on, we still can praise and celebrate on our way.

DAY 28

Look not every man on his own things,
but every man also on the things of others.
Philippians 2:4

I live in the San Francisco Bay Area. Downtown San Francisco is one of the worst places to park. To find a parking space you have to have the patience of Job and the luck of the Irish. So I circled the block for what seemed like an eternity.

Finally I caught someone coming out of a parking space. As I approached the meter I noticed that there was still over an hour left on the meter. As a result I didn't have to put any money in the meter.

Someone had paid the price before me. We all need someone to help us. We ought to be grateful for the people who have paid the price and sacrificed before us, allowing us to experience things that we never had to pay a price for.

Even Jesus Himself paid the price for us at Calvary, allowing us to reap the benefits of the ultimate price He paid for with His life.

DAY 29

But seek first the kingdom of God and
all these things will be added unto you
Matthew 6:33

When one gets on a glass elevator you can see everything clear and distinctly on the ground floor.

But as you elevate higher and higher, the things that are on the ground get smaller and smaller.

As you elevate your life in Christ the things and the desires of this world get smaller and smaller the higher you go.

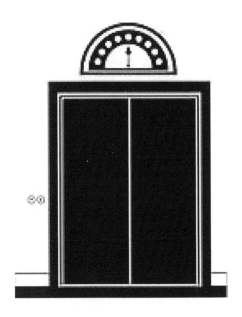

DAY 30

One of my prized possessions as a boy was my own record player. Though I only had three 45s, I played them over and over as if it was the first time I had ever heard the record.

To play a 45rpm record, you needed something known as a "Spider" which was an adapter that helps the record remain in the center of the turntable. If you didn't possess the Spider, the record would not stay in the center and it would be impossible to play.

We must always make sure that God remains at the center of our lives.

DAY 31

Behold, I will do a new thing; now it shall spring forth; shall ye not know it? I will even make a way in the wilderness, and rivers in the desert.

Isaiah 43:19

It is a fact that a good, hot iron and spray starch helps get the wrinkles out of clothes. When you spray starch from a can it makes that *ssshhhhh!* sound. I was ironing a shirt and using spray starch and I heard the familiar *sssshhhhh!* sound as I sprayed.

But as I continued to iron I was not achieving the normal result; my shirt was still wrinkled. It was making the normal sound but achieving no results.

Sometimes we can do something so long that we don't even notice that it is not effective anymore. We are going through the motions and exerting energy but with no results.

DAY 32

Iron sharpeneth iron;
so a man sharpeneth the countenance of his friend.
Proverbs 27:17

In elementary school we took turns reading out loud. I prided myself on being a good reader, and would anticipate my turn to read. After reading my paragraphs I loved to hear my teacher say that I received an "A" for the reading that day.

But there was another classmate of mine who had a stuttering problem and as he began to read I laughed at his stuttering. My teacher heard me laughing and became very angry.

She said, "Brian, since you are laughing at your classmate, I'm going to give him another chance tomorrow, and I expect you to help him. I am going to erase your "A" and whatever grade he gets tomorrow, that's the grade you are going to get."

Even though we are successful, we must always find a way to help and not hinder.

DAY 33

All things work together for our good,
to them who love God and are called
according to his purpose
Romans 8:28

I love real buttermilk ranch dressing. Ranch dressing on salad, on french fries, on baked potatoes, and even buffalo wings. I love real buttermilk ranch dressing! Though I love buttermilk ranch dressing, I detest one of its main ingredients: buttermilk! I detest the smell and texture of it.

Though I would never drink buttermilk by itself, when it is mixed with the other ingredients it is a wonderful condiment.

We may not like the individual problems that we encounter, but when we allow God to mix it in with the ups and downs, successes and defeats, we ultimately see how all - not just one, but all - things are working together for our good.

DAY 34

He who began a good work in you
will perform it until the day of Jesus Christ
Philippians 1:6

My grandmother was an accomplished seamstress. As a seamstress, she would cut away fabric to form a pattern. The pieces that she cut away she called remnants. They looked like scraps fit for the trash to me.

But instead of throwing away the scraps she would collect and save them. Believe it or not, from those scraps she could make an entire quilt. As she made the quilt it had two sides; one side looked like a hodgepodge mess, but the other side looked like a tapestry masterpiece. The side you looked at defined your perspective and reaction.

Depending on how you look at life, sometimes it can look like a hodgepodge mess. But other times, if we look at the other side it can look like it's all together, neatly arranged.

DAY 35

Forgetting those things that are behind
and reaching forth to those things which are before
Philippians 3:12

Upon entering my credit union to transact some business, I had to walk through a peculiar corridor. I walked into the door only to find another door in front of me. I tried to push the other door open and it would not budge.

But I noticed as the first door closed behind me then immediately the door in front of me opened. I couldn't go forward until the door behind me had closed completely.

Before we can move forward we have to close the door to our past, allowing the door of our future to open so we can move forward.

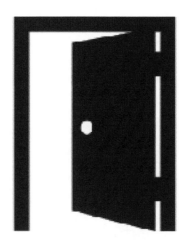

DAY 36

For my thoughts are not your thoughts, neither are your ways my ways, saith the LORD.
Isaiah 55:8

A little girl decided to get up early and fix breakfast for her mother and father. She spent quite some time banging pots, mixing ingredients, etc. When her father finally came into the kitchen it was a mess! But the little girl asked him to read the note on the kitchen counter which read: I know things seem like they are a mess now, but I'm working on something.

Life can seem a mess sometimes, but God's word assures that in the midst of the mess, He leaves us a note that He is working on something.

DON'T FORGET YOUR S.O.A.P.

- **Scripture**

Write down what stuck out to you in your reading.

- **Observation**

What did you observe about the scripture that struck you. This can be one sentence or a whole book.

- **Application**

How can you apply the observation so that it affects your life today.

- **Prayer**

Write out a prayer to God based on what you just learned and ask him to help you apply this truth in your life.

Day 37

Draw near to God and He will draw near to you

James 4:8

I never will forget the love of my life in fifth grade. Her
name was Paige. I remember her vividly. Big, shiny afro,
soft, smooth skin, bangle bracelets on her wrist, and she
always smelled like cinnamon. Our fifth grade class went to
a nearby amusement park, and I had the privilege of
having Paige as my girlfriend for the day.

I wasn't content with us just walking together - I wanted to
hold her hand, but I could not figure out a way to get her
close enough to do so.
We got on our first roller coaster together, she sat on her
side and I sat on mine. Still praying for her to be close to
me, the Lord answered my prayer. As the roller coaster
began to make twists and turns, the centrifugal force began
to work to my advantage. Paige just slid right over to me! If
it wasn't for the twists and turns we would have never
gotten so close.

God will use the twists and turns and the ups and downs of
life to bring us closer to him.

DAY 38

For I know the plans I have for you, declares the Lord, plans for welfare and not for evil, to give you a future and a hope.
Jeremiah 29:11

When my oldest daughter, Imanni, was a little girl she loved to ride her tricycle. She didn't know how to pedal yet so she would just put her feet on the pedals and hands on the handlebars.

Luckily I did not have to bend over to push her, because there was long steering handle attached to the back of the tricycle and I could walk upright and push the tricycle.

My daughter thought because she had her hands on the handlebars she was really steering and determining where she was going. She thought that she was really controlling the pace because she had her feet on the pedals. But because I had the steering handle behind her I controlled everything. It appeared to her that she was in control, but in reality I was controlling everything.

It may look and feel like we are in control, but behind the scenes God is still in complete control.

DAY 39

I admit that visiting the dentist is not on the top of my list. The sound of the instruments grinding is not one of my favorite sounds to hear. I was having tremendous pain with one of my teeth, and I kept trying to medicate that pain with ibuprofen, but to no avail.

The pain was relentless and I had to go to the dentist. It was decided that my wisdom tooth needed to be pulled. The dentist began to numb the tooth and made his first attempt to pull it out. Yet I could still feel tremendous pain. He administered more anesthesia and made another attempt. I could still feel the pain. He gave me more anesthetic and made yet another attempt. Still the pain was unbearable.

He couldn't understand why I still felt pain; after all his attempts the tooth was very numb. What he discovered was that the tooth was so infected that it was blocking the anesthesia. The tooth wasn't in a state to be pulled.

There may be areas of our lives that can become so "infected" that the Word of God even has problems penetrating the areas where we need help the most.

DAY 40

Commit thy way unto the LORD; trust also in him;
and he shall bring it to pass
Psalm 37:5

My son and I set out one Saturday to fly a kite. He chose a box kite. I only had experience putting together the normal, conventional diamond kite. The box kite was a little different. It had intricate design, multiple pieces, and I actually had to read the directions.

What I thought would be done easily and quick was time consuming and meticulous. All the while my son kept asking, "Is it ready yet?" to which I responded by saying very politely, "No, almost." More time would go by and he would ask again, "Is the kite ready yet?" Getting a little annoyed now because of my frustration in trying to put the kite together, I now replied, "Not yet! I will tell you when."

All the while I am working, sweating, reading the directions, redoing things I thought were right. All the while he is skipping, jumping, and singing and never asked if he could help me. He let me handle it and kept asking was it ready yet? When I finished he had no idea what it took to put it together, but he flew the kite high in the sky with a smile on his face.

While God is working some things out on our behalf, we ought to let Him do the work and follow the example of my son; singing praise with anticipation while He works.

DAY 41

Thy word is a light unto my path
and a lamp unto my feet
Psalm 119:105

In California there is a stretch of highway called Highway 5. Highway 5 is a flat highway running through long stretches of agricultural fields. Although there are many rest stops and gas stations on Highway 5 they are stretched out over long distances.

I was traveling Highway 5 with a friend of mine and we made a stop and I recommended that we get gas, but he insisted that we didn't need to. So we got back on the road and after about fifteen minutes on the road the gas light came on. I became very nervous because the next gas station wasn't at least for another twenty-five miles, and there aren't any emergency call boxes on Highway 5. So I began to panic because I didn't want to run out of gas.

He suggested that I grab the owner's manual and see just how far we could go once the gas light came on. I discovered that we could go thirty-five miles after the gas warning light came on. Though we didn't know just how far we could go, the manual assured us that we could go a little further and that we were going to make it.
Just when you think that you cannot go any further and you are about to "run out of gas" our owner's manual, the Bible, assures us that we can go a little while longer and we will make it!

DAY 42

Restore to me the joy of your salvation,
and uphold me with a willing spirit.
Psalm 51:12

Years ago I was dating a young lady who wore her hair very short. I remember dropping her off at the beauty salon and upon picking her up, as she walked to the car I didn't even recognize her because now she had long hair to the middle of her back. She went in with hardly any hair but came out with long, black locks. Of course in my amazement, I enquired as to how this happened.

She explained to me that she got what is called a weave. What I learned is for a weave to be successful you have to have enough hair for the beautician to grab in between her fingers.

The beautician then takes synthetic hair and weaves it into your real hair. If the beautician is good you can't tell where the real hair and fake hair is weaved. But all she needs is just a little bit to start with and she can do wonders.

No matter what we may have lost or feel we don't have, God can take what little bit we may possess and add to it. He can add to it and make it better.

DAY 43

Fret not thyself because of evildoers
Psalm 37:1

Though I am terribly afraid of snakes, I am intrigued by their habits and characteristics in the wild. I learned a great deal about snakes from the late Steve Irwin, better known as the "Crocodile Hunter".

He instructs us never to run if you encounter a snake. As difficult as it may be, stand completely still. He says snakes only strike at objects that are moving.

All of us have "snakes" in our lives. Some "snakes" come in the form of enemies, even friends or colleagues. As long as we are standing still, our "snakes" really don't manifest themselves though they are all around. It is only when we begin to make progress and move forward, pursuing dreams and goals, that they manifest themselves, trying to impede our progress.

DAY 44

Where there is no vision the people perish

Proverbs 29:18

Steve Irwin, the late, great zoologist, taught me another valuable lesson regarding snakes. He informed me that snakes don't have ears, but rather they use their forked tongues as "ears" to sense what is around them.
When he pointed that out I had to look twice because in all these years I guess I never really paid much attention. But he is right; they don't have ears. So they really can't hear.

You know you are dealing with a "snake" in your life because no matter how much you talk they don't hear you. "I told you I don't like that," or "I have told you time and time again I don't like to be treated like that." Or for leaders, they don't hear or see your vision. They aren't hearing you because snakes don't have ears.

DAY 45

Do not rejoice when your enemy falls,
and let not your heart be glad when he stumbles
Proverbs 24:17

It is a fact that snakes are cold blooded animals. They are looking for warmth and heat to sun in. They cannot make heat themselves, so they depend on the heat from another source to keep them warm.

Be careful of those who don't have their own "sun"; their own dreams and goals. They will try to warm themselves from your "sun".

REMEMBER TO USE YOUR S.O.A.P.

- **Scripture**

Write down what stuck out to you in your reading.

- **Observation**

What did you observe about the scripture that struck you. This can be one sentence or a whole book.

- **Application**

How can you apply the observation so that it affects your life today.

- **Prayer**

Write out a prayer to God based on what you just learned and ask him to help you apply this truth in your life.

DAY 46

He chose us in Him before the foundation of the world, that we would be holy and blameless before Him In love

Ephesians 1:4

I love watching documentaries that depict animals in their natural habitat. One documentary highlighted both apes and waterbirds in their natural habitat. Both animals lived and thrived in trees, and both lived near water. Though they were both exposed to water, they each had a very different reaction to water.

The ape was terrified of water and stayed as far away as he could from it. But the duck thrived in water. What was the difference? Though they both were exposed to the same elements, the duck was built and equipped for the water and the ape simply was not. So the duck thrived in an environment that would ultimately take the ape under.

As believers we may be in the same environment as others, but we can thrive in environments where others may be taken under. We may be equipped to handle an environment that others simply cannot. Moses and Joseph were both in Egypt; Egypt was a burden to Moses but Joseph thrived in Egypt.

DAY 47

Trust in the Lord with all your heart, and do not lean on your own understanding. In all your ways acknowledge him, and he will make straight your paths.
Proverbs 3:5-6

A scientist climbed to a lofty height to look over a skyscraper banister. He wanted to see how different things responded to being dropped from the same height.

He dropped a plate and as soon as it hit the ground it shattered into a million pieces. He then dropped a bag of flour and it hit the ground with a loud *thud!* and just laid there. He then dropped a ball and it bounced back up and down several times before coming to a stop. They were each dropped from the same height but each had a different result as they landed. Each item responded to being dropped based on what was on the inside of them and what they were made of.

We may encounter the same problems and circumstances as someone else. The circumstance does not matter. What matters is how we respond to the circumstance. We can fall to pieces like that plate, lay dead as the bag of flour, or we can bounce back like that ball from each and every circumstance. Because we have the Holy Ghost dwelling on the inside we have what it takes to bounce back every time. There is a classic spiritual song that says, "There is something within that holds the reins, something within that banishes pain, something within I cannot explain. All I know is there is something within."

DAY 48

I know both how to be abased, and I know how to abound: every where and in all things I am instructed both to be full and to be hungry, both to abound and to suffer need.

Philippians 4:12

In my early teens I discovered I had a gift for running track. I became so good that I never lost a race from seventh grade to my sophomore year in high school. I didn't know what it meant to lose. With that kind of winning streak, I became very arrogant and cocky. My dad admonished me time and time again to remain humble but to no avail; I remained cocky as ever.

So my dad decided to teach me a lesson. I was running on the Junior Varsity team, and my dad asked my coach to allow me to run one meet at the Varsity level. In my arrogance, I surmised that it really didn't matter what level it was, I was going to win. I entered the race overconfident as in times past. As the race transpired I found myself slipping behind. At first by just a little and then by a lot! I could literally see the back of my opponents as they left me in the dust. I ran as fast as I could but fell further behind. I was embarrassed as I came in a miserable sixth place.

After the race I literally had a temper tantrum melt down. My attitude was terrible! My dad came out to the infield to straighten me out. He informs me that he told the coach to put me in a varsity race, and I demanded (gently of course) why he would do such a thing? He replied that I needed to know how to handle myself not just as a winner, but I also needed to know how to handle my losses. He said, "Son, you learn more from your losses than you do from your wins." After that, needless to say I was so much more humble and learned how to respond to my losses.

Our Heavenly Father wants to make sure we are balanced; that we would know how to handle good success, but also know how to handle and balance disappointments and losses. On purpose he gives us both. Paul says, "I have learned how to both be abased and abound. How to be in full and how to be in want."

DAY 49

Be still and know that I am God

Psalm 46:10

A young woman was kidnapped from a grocery store parking lot, pulled into a van, and driven to a remote location in the woods. She was beaten and raped, wrapped in duct tape from head to toe and thrown in a ditch to die.

To make matters worse, as she was lying in the ditch trapped in duct tape, it began to rain.

Fortunately she survived the ordeal. After she was found and rescued they interviewed her and asked how she survived. She recounted how she was trapped in duct tape and she could not move or scream and it began to rain. At first she thought that it couldn't get any worse than what it was and now it's raining?

But the rain was what actually saved her life; it began to loosen the duct tape which allowed her to free her hands and feet to get help. So the storm actually saved her life. Though it may not seem like it, the storms of our lives can actually work to our advantage. What seems like a problem can really be a stepping stone that will work for our good.

DAY 50

The thief does not come except to steal kill and destroy.
I have come that they may have life,
and that they may have it more abundantly
John 10:10

New Zealand news headlines tells the story of a Shrek the sheep, who became famous several years ago when he was found after hiding out in caves for six years. Of course, during this time his fleece grew without anyone there to shear (shave) it. When he was finally found and shaved, his fleece weighed an amazing sixty pounds. Most sheep have fleece weighing just under ten pounds, with the exception usually reaching fifteen pounds, maximum.

For six years, Shrek carried six times the regular weight of his fleece, simply because he was away from his shepherd. When Shrek was found, a professional sheep shearer took care of Shrek's fleece in twenty-eight minutes. Shrek's sixty-pound fleece was finally removed. All it took was coming home to his shepherd.

This reminds me of John 10 when Jesus compares Himself to a shepherd, and His followers are His sheep. Shrek is much like a person who knows Jesus Christ but has wandered. If we avoid Christ's constant refining of our character, we're going to accumulate extra weight in this world—a weight we don't have to bear. Christ can lift the burdens we carry, if only we stop hiding. He can shave off our 'fleece'—that is, our self-imposed burdens brought about by wandering from our Good Shepherd.

DAY 51

*And let us not be weary in well doing: f
or in due season we shall reap, if we faint not
Galatians 6:9*

A friend of mine took his dream vacation in Dubai at a five star resort. He thoroughly enjoyed himself and had the time of his life. But something really threw him off.

In the five star resort every so often the lights would flicker as if they were going to go out. He discovered that because of where the resort was, electricity was hard to maintain. When the lights flicker they are really on the verge of going out, but there is generator in the basement of the hotel that kicks in just before the lights go out.

There are times when it looks like we may flicker out and give up because of the experience of what we may be going through. But because the Holy Spirit dwells on the inside, even when we want to give up, He gives us the strength to allow us to stand and not give up.

DAY 52

Therefore do not be anxious about tomorrow, for tomorrow will be anxious for itself. Sufficient for the day is its own trouble.
Matthew 6:34

It can be very frustrating to be working on a computer project, and all of sudden out of nowhere an annoying ad pops up. Pop ups are a nuisance because they pop up right in the middle of the screen covering and blocking the very thing I am working on.
The remedy is a pop up blocker; a software program that prevents any unexpected pop ups from coming onto your screen thereby preventing your work. Unbeknownst to us at times God has blocked things in our life to limit our distractions and help us to be as productive as we can.

ALWAYS USE YOUR S.O.A.P.

· **Scripture**
Write down what stuck out to you in your reading.

· **Observation**
What did you observe about the scripture that struck you. This can be one sentence or a whole book.

· **Application**
How can you apply the observation so that it affects your life today.

· **Prayer**
Write out a prayer to God based on what you just learned and ask him to help you apply this truth in your life.

Day 53

Therefore if any man be in Christ, he is a new creature: old things are passed away; behold, all things are become new.

2 Corinthians 5:17

Witnessing a space shuttle take off is literally breathtaking. As it lifts off the engines are spewing fire and combustion as it is climbs higher and higher. As it moves into outer space and reaches a certain altitude certain things begin to fall off the spacecraft as well.

The higher it goes the lighter it becomes. It cannot have certain limitations and weight as it reaches new heights.

As we go higher reaching different levels and heights in our lives, there are people and other limitations that must be taken off if we are to soar to the heights that we are destined.

DAY 54

On August 25, 2001 the world was shocked to hear that the young R&B singing sensation known as Aliyah had been killed in an airplane crash. In a hurry to get back to the U.S. from the Bahamas the plane was overloaded with crew and equipment.

Upon takeoff the plane was too heavy to get the proper liftoff and crashed to the ground. The plane never reached its destined altitude because of its weight.

We must be careful that we are not overloaded by people, thoughts, and our own limitations that we never reach the destination we were intended to reach.

DAY 55

Let them praise the name of the LORD, For His name alone is exalted; His glory is above earth and heaven.

Psalm 148:13

Vince Lombardi undoubtedly will go down as one of the best coaches in football history. Upon taking the helm of the Green Bay Packers, they had come off a 0-11 losing streak.

After taking leadership of the team, they never had another losing season. They went on to be Super Bowl champions time and time over. The influence of one man turned everything around. Sometimes the influence of one person in our lives can turn everything around.

DAY 56

For I the LORD thy God will hold thy right hand
saying unto thee fear not I will help you
Isaiah 41:13

Because there is no gravity in space after an expedition the astronauts have to relearn how to walk and do normal activities again. Because they had been in an environment where there was no resistance, it actually proved to be detrimental to them.

So they developed suits that would mirror the gravitational resistance to keep the astronauts familiar with normal resistance in pull. Resistance is necessary.

DAY 57

Until 2007 there had never been an NFL team who had won a Super Bowl whose home field had a domed stadium. The football teams who had a domed stadium were always used to playing in perfect conditions, so when they had to play in Buffalo in the snow facing freezing temperatures or the sweltering heat of Florida or Los Angeles, they struggled.

God loves us enough to make sure the conditions in our lives are not perfect. He knows if we are to be the best that we can be, we must have sunshine and rain.

DAY 58

In Exodus 30 God gives the ingredients for the anointing oil that will be used in anointing ceremonies. He names Cassia, Calamus. Cinnamon, myrrh, and olive oil. What is interesting is that the anointing oil symbolic of the Holy Spirit was made up of bitter ingredients and sweet ingredients.

You could not have the true anointing oil with just bitter ingredients, and you could not have it with just sweet ingredients. There must be a combination of both. To be truly anointed and empowered by the Spirit there will be some sweet times and some bitter times in our lives. We must have both. "I have learned in whatsoever state I am in to be content. I know how to be up and I know how to be down."

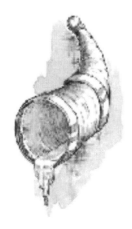

DAY 59

For everything there is a season, and a time for every matter under heaven

Ecclesiastes 3:1

Listening to one of my favorite preachers, she made note of how God took his time to bring out certain gifts in her. She declared how God waited till she was in her thirties to call her to preach. He waited till she was in her forties to call her into the pastorate, and into her fifties for her to be an author. Never think that it is too late for God to do something in your life. God is not in a hurry and He will ultimately pull out what is inside of you.

DAY 60

Though a host should camp against me
my heart shall not fear
Psalm 27:3

Though I am not fond of the smell of fertilizer, I am surprised by its purpose. Fertilizer is manure that is processed and used to grow plants.

There are properties in the fertilizer that help the plants grow faster. Though none of us want to be in a mess, drama, chaos, or confusion, there are time when "mess" helps us to grow a little faster.

DAY 61

Evildoers shall be cut off but those that wait on the Lord shall inherit the earth

Psalm 37:9

A number of years back the codfish industry on the northeast coast of the US had a problem. How could they keep the codfish fresh while they transported them across the country? When they froze the fish they lost too much flavor. When they transported them live in tanks filled with saltwater the fish got soft and mushy.

Finally they found a solution. They placed catfish in the tanks with the codfish. Catfish are a natural enemy of codfish, so the catfish would chase them around the tanks all the time they were being transported. The cod now arrived in better condition than ever because the constant motion helped them remain fresh. We all need catfish in our lives – the difficult people or situations in life that may not be pleasant but keep us healthy and growing.

DAY 62

When you have done all to stand; Stand!

Ephesians 6:13

The La Torre Pisa, commonly known as the Leaning Tower of Pisa, has eight stories, and it leans forty-five degrees. It has been leaning for 840 years and has never fallen down. It has defied the laws of gravity and is still standing.

You may be leaning because of all the problems, trials, and difficulties you have been through. But thank God that after all you have been through you are still standing.

DAY 63

. . . Forgiving each other; as the Lord has forgiven you,
so you also must forgive
Colossians 3:13

A parishioner came to her pastor because she didn't know how to forgive. He took her up to the bell tower, handed her the rope and asked her to ring the church bell. She rang it quite a few times and then he told her to let go of the rope.

The bell rang for a few more minutes of its own accord and then it stopped. The pastor said, "That's how you forgive.

As long as you have your hand on what the person did, you will be reminded of the offense. Forgiveness is taking your hand off of the offense. You may still feel the ring for a while but eventually it will stop."

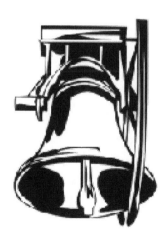

DAY 64

Trust in the Lord with all thine heart and lean not to your own understanding. In all your ways acknowledge him and he shall direct the paths.

Proverbs 3:5-6

After graduating high school, I had the opportunity to visit Germany. While there we visited a botanical garden. In the middle of the garden was a huge maze of hedges that were fifteen feet tall. We decided to walk through the maze. Some of my colleagues walked through it, easily finding the outlet.

Once you had made it through, you could go up on a high platform and look down at others making their way through the maze. Navigating the maze was a little difficult for me and to make matters worse it was getting dark. I didn't want to be stuck in the maze alone. The only way I made it through the maze was by listening to the voice of the people above me, who could see the outlay of the maze and instructed me to the outlet.

DAY 65

For I reckon that the sufferings of this present time are not worthy to be compared with the glory which shall be revealed in us
Romans 8:18

One of my fondest childhood memories is spending time at my grandmother's house. Her house always smelled like fresh flowers. Every few days she would adorn her dining room table with flowers. When the flowers started to wilt I expected her to thrown them in the trash. But instead she would take the petals off the stem and crush them in a bowl and place them all over the house.

Though they looked dead on the stem, as she crushed them they released a fragrance that still filled the room though they looked like they were dead. We may feel/look like it's all over, but God has a way of crushing us to the degree where there is still something left.

DAY 66

For it is God which worketh in you
both to will and to do of his good pleasure
Philippians 2:13

My mother taught me a valuable lesson regarding a tube of toothpaste. I was going to discard a tube of toothpaste, my mother stopped me and asked why was I throwing toothpaste away? I said, "There is no more in there." She said, "Yes there is."

She took the toothpaste and began rolling and squeezing the tube from the bottom and, lo and behold, there was a whole lot more toothpaste in there. Just when you think that it's all over God can squeeze more out of you and the situation.

DAY 67

For our gospel came not unto you in word only
but also in power and in the Holy Ghost
1 Thessalonians 1:5

Before there were laws in place, I remember as a little boy I could buy cigarettes. My aunt would send me to the local store with a note. All I did was give the note to the storekeeper and put the money on the counter.

Without exchanging a word he would read the note, take the money, and hand me the cigarettes. Though the store keeper never saw my aunt, the authority was in the note she wrote and I simply read what was on the note. As a preacher I read the "note", the Bible, as God said it. It carries authority because He said it.

DAY 68

. . . but David encouraged himself in the LORD his God
1 Samuel 30:6

As my son began to learn how to walk, he would take a step or two and we would get so excited and clap for him. Every time he would take a step we would clap and make a big deal of it. I remember one time he took some steps and no one clapped for him.

He paused for a moment waiting for the applause and when no one did, he just started clapping for himself. Sometimes you can't wait for others to encourage you. Sometimes you have to encourage yourself.

DAY 69

When I was a child, I spoke like a child, I thought like a child, I reasoned like a child. When I became a man, I gave up childish ways
1 Corinthians 13:11

All of my kids enjoyed coloring in coloring books. When they started they would use several different colors and they would never stay inside the lines. Though it was a hodgepodge mess I would still say how wonderful the picture was.

As they "matured" they learned to use the proper colors and stay inside the lines, and I could see a vast improvement. Many of us know what it's like to be disobedient outside the lines, but as we mature we learn to stay in the lines as He has asked us to.

KEEP USING YOUR S.O.A.P.

• **Scripture**
Write down what stuck out to you in your reading.

• **Observation**
What did you observe about the scripture that struck you. This can be one sentence or a whole book.

• **Application**
How can you apply the observation so that it affects your life today.

• **Prayer**
Write out a prayer to God based on what you just learned and ask him to help you apply this truth in your life.

DAY 70

not forsaking our own assembling together,
as is the habit of some, but encouraging one another;
and all the more as you see the day drawing near
Hebrews 10:25

I was an avid fan of the prizefighter Mike Tyson. He was hailed as a knockout artist. But I noticed as he was on his way to the ring there was a guy who was beside him the whole way, encouraging him. "You're the best, Mike." "Nobody like you, Mike." "You gonna get 'em tonight, Mike." But even when Mike Tyson lost, on his way from the ring the same guy was at his shoulder encouraging him. Whether we are up or down, winning or losing, we all need someone to encourage us.

DAY 71

Lift up your hands in the sanctuary, and bless the LORD
Psalm 134:2

I remember helping all of my kids when they were small to take their shirts off at the end of the day. When I would lift the shirt above their heads sometimes it got stuck. They couldn't see anything because the shirt was covering their face. As a result they began to struggle. I would admonish them to raise your arms! raise your arms!

As long as they struggled and left their face and arms in the shirt they were confined. But as soon as they raised their arms I was able to lift the shirt right off. We struggle with things, and God is waiting for us to lift our arms in surrender to Him. When we surrender, He is able to take the burden away.

DAY 72

Do not be anxious about anything, but in everything
by prayer and supplication with thanksgiving
let your requests be made known to God.
Philippians 4:6-7

Nobody likes to be under pressure. Pressure to meet a deadline, pressure to make a decision, etc. Oftentimes we think that pressure is negative. However, the tires on a car have to have pressure. Without pressure they would be flat and would not be able to take the car where it should go.

Sometimes pressure is needed. as it allows us to go from one place to the others.

DAY 73

Bless the LORD, O my soul:
and all that is within me, bless his holy name.
Psalm 103:1

"Barak" is the Hebrew word for bless, which means to kneel. The word bless is a word that comes out of the culture of the times. As some travelers would go from place to place they traveled with camels who bore their wares.

When they reached their destination they couldn't reach the top of the camel to get the stuff off his back. So they would take a stick and begin to hit the knees of the camel and yell "Barak! Barak!" The camel would eventually fall to its knees, thereby making it easy to get the burdens off his back.

We too can have things that we are burdened down by. As long as we stand in our own pride and strength we will shoulder the burdens. But when we kneel in submission He is able to take the burdens off of us.

DAY 74

The steps of a good man are ordered by the LORD
Psalm 37:23

Alfred Hitchcock is known as one of the best suspense directors in the business. But if you look closely, he makes cameo appearances in a number of his films. But you have to look close to really notice that he is in the picture.

For example, in the "The Birds" he can be seen winding a clock. In "Dial M for Murder" he can be seen walking a dog. Though he was the director behind the scenes, he could also be seen in the middle of the action.
Though God is the director, He can also be seen in the action of our lives, though sometimes we have to really look to see His face and hand in the action.

DON'T FORGET YOUR S.O.A.P.

• **Scripture**
Write down what stuck out to you in your reading.

• **Observation**
What did you observe about the scripture that struck you. This can be one sentence or a whole book.

• **Application**
How can you apply the observation so that it affects your life today.

• **Prayer**
Write out a prayer to God based on what you just learned and ask him to help you apply this truth in your life.

DAY 75

Thus will I bless thee while I live: I will lift up my hands in thy name.

One of my favorite movies is a comedy entitled "Life". "Life" is the story about two friends, Claude and Ray. They were framed for a crime that they didn't commit and sentenced to life in prison.

Time and time again they plot several failed escape attempts, until one day Claude sets the infirmary on fire and runs into it as if he is trying to save Ray.

The last time we see Claude and Ray they are in the fire headed to their deaths. But in the very next scene we see them in Yankee Stadium with their hands lifted and cheering.

DAY 76

Oh give thanks to the LORD, call upon His name;
Make known His deeds among the peoples
1 Chronicles 16:8

Growing up I was never one to like to fight. However, my sister never ran from a fight. She had a reputation in our neighborhood and as a result no one really messed with her.

I remember going to the corner store, buying a big bag of candy. On the way back I was confronted by the neighborhood bully who was trying to snatch my bag of candy. I was panicked and afraid. Tears began to swell in my eyes.

It was then that I had a bright idea. I just began to yell my sister's name. Though he couldn't see her, he knew of her reputation. I knew she wasn't home but he didn't. I kept calling her name and finally he ran off. There is a name that is above every name! The name of the Lord is a strong tower.

DAY 77

O LORD our Lord, how excellent is thy name in all the earth! who hast set thy glory above the heavens
Psalm 8:1

Upon reading the biography of Steve Jobs it was interesting to note that though he was one of the founders of the Apple, he was fired from his own company.

Steve Jobs was the innovator and creator of several Apple products. Once they let him go they discovered that profits and innovations were at an all time low. They decided to ask him back, and almost overnight profits began to soar because they had the creator back in his place.

DAY 78

Likewise the Spirit helps us in our weakness. For we do not know what to pray for as we ought, but the Spirit himself intercedes for us with groanings too deep for words

Romans 8:26

There is an old story about a world famous organist. To play the organ, air had to be pumped into the organ as he pressed the keys. The famous organist played the first half of a concert to a thunderous applause.

The famous organist went backstage and said to the man who was responsible for pumping air into the organ, "Man, those people sure do love me!" His assistant said, "Don't you mean they loved us?" The organist responded, "No, those people are clapping for me. I just played a masterpiece." His assistant didn't argue with him.

As the organist went for the next set of the concert, he sat at the bench and put his fingers on the keys. When he pressed them, nothing came out. He pressed again and still nothing happened. The people who were cheering were now laughing and jeering.

He said to his assistant, "Man, we got a show to do, start pumping the air!" to which the assistant replied, "Well you did so well the first time without me, I just thought that you would do it again."
We never succeed by ourselves. We always need the help of someone else.

DAY 79

God has not given us a spirit of fear
but of love, power, and a sound mind
2 Timothy 1:7

There was an aspiring dancer whose sole dream was to dance on Broadway. She practiced for hours upon hours, hoping that someday she would grace the stage.

One day her friends got together and discouraged her so badly that not only did she give up dancing, but she also decided to commit suicide. So she went to the Golden Gate Bridge and before she jumped off she began to write a suicide note that began by saying "They said . . ." After writing it she jumped to her death.

When the police got there all they found was a note that read "They said . . ." The morning headline for the *San Francisco Chronicle* read "Young aspiring dancer jumps to her death; cause unknown, but something they said made her do it." Sometimes you can't listen to what they say.

DAY 80

*If we confess our sins, he is faithful and just to forgive us our sins,
and to cleanse us from all unrighteousness*
1 John 1:9

An old story is told of a little boy who loved to throw rocks in the yard. Time and time again he was told by his mother, "Son, don't throw rocks." Despite her admonition he continued to throw rocks. One day he threw a rock and hit and killed his mother's prized duck.

He thought no one saw him until dinner time was over and his sister said, "If you don't do the dishes for me, I am gonna tell mother about the duck." For an entire week his sister made him do chores and if he refused she would say, "Remember the duck?"

After two long weeks of being enslaved by his sister who was holding the mistake over his head, he couldn't take it anymore. He ran to his mother and confessed that he had killed the duck. After his tearful confession his mother said, "Son, I saw you when you did it. I was just waiting for you to come and tell me you did it so I could forgive you."

DAY 81

For nothing will be impossible with God
Luke 1:37

I had a friend in high school who loved Mercedes Benz cars. Every day he would wear a Mercedes Benz hat. We would ridicule him from time to time because he wore a Mercedes hat but didn't own a Mercedes. Later he not only donned the hat but he also secured a key chain, and we continued to ridicule him. After graduation, still in our caps and gowns, we looked in disbelief as Barry sat in a brand new Mercedes Benz.

Unbeknownst to us Barry was told by his father that if he achieved a certain GPA upon graduation he would buy him a Mercedes Benz. Though he didn't have the car yet, he was already acting like it. So when he got the car the hat and the key chain were already in place.

DAY 82

Beloved, now are we the sons of God, and it doth not yet appear what we shall be: but we know that, when he shall appear, we shall be like him; for we shall see him as he is

1 John 3:2

In high school I was the 400 meter league champion two years in row. I have competed overseas in places such as Germany and Holland. However, my track and field career didn't start so well. In sixth and seventh grade, I literally lost every race.

After the race, my dad would say, "Don't worry about it, there is a winner in you." That sounded ridiculous to me because surely he had seen that I had just lost the race, and yet he had the audacity to say I was a winner?

But from eighth grade to my senior year in high school I never lost a race. After my last race as a senior, my dad reminded me that he had known there was a winner in me. Though I couldn't see it, he always could see the best in me.

DAY 83

I am the way, the truth, and the life

John 14:6

Many of us witnessed the meteoric rise to fame of Britney Spears. We also witnessed how her life began to spiral out of control based on that same success. Her life was out of control, and it seemed like no one could get to her.

That is until her father stepped onto the scene. Her father actually moved in with her, went where she went, and took control of her affairs. After her father moved in her life began to change for the better.

DAY 84

Be strong, and let your heart take courage,
all you who wait for the Lord
Psalm 31:24

One night while watching Monday night football, the legendary coach and commentator John Madden witnessed the running back expertise of Emmitt Smith. Upon witnessing Smith's prowess, he actually invented a new statistical category for him. John Madden invented a category called "YAC", which stands for "yards after contact."
Emmitt Smith was not only known for how many yards he achieved but also how many yards he was able to achieve after being hit.

GOT S.O.A.P. ?

- **Scripture**
Write down what stuck out to you in your reading.

- **Observation**
What did you observe about the scripture that struck you. This can be one sentence or a whole book.

- **Application**
How can you apply the observation so that it affects your life today.

- **Prayer**
Write out a prayer to God based on what you just learned and ask him to help you apply this truth in your life.

DAY 85

Put on the whole armor of God, that you may be able to stand against the schemes of the devil

Ephesians 6:11

A moose spends a great deal of time eating in the summer, for he knows in the fall there is a mating battle. The strongest bucks get to mate. So the moose knows in order to get ready for the battle in the fall, he must prepare in the summer.

He can't get ready for the battle in the fall, he must be prepared beforehand. We can't wait for the enemy to attack and then prepare. We must prepare beforehand.

DAY 86

1 removed the burden from their shoulders; their hands were set free from the basket. In your distress you called and 1 rescued you

Psalm 81:6-7

Ants can carry one hundred times their body weight. An ant was carrying a piece of straw. He approached a large gap in the sidewalk, and after circling for a while he did something genius.

He took the piece of straw out of his mouth and laid it across the gap and walked over it. Once he was on the other side he picked up the straw and continued to move on.

DAY 87

Do not withhold good from those to whom it is due,
when it is in your power to do it
Proverbs 3:27

My son participated in his first track meet when he was five years of age. Being a former track and field star, I gave him as many pointers as I could. He was slated to run the 50 yard dash. I was proud to watch him win his race.

After his race, in the next heat, I witnessed something I had never seen in track and field history. Two little girls were running side by side, matching each other stride for stride.

Then all of a sudden one of the girls tripped and fell. The rest of the runners kept going towards the finish line. The girl who is running next to the girl who fell stopped and went back to help the girl get up. They ran to the finish line together amid cheers of surprise and encouragement.

DAY 88

Rejoice in hope, be patient in tribulation, be constant in prayer

Romans 12:12

Growing up I was very familiar with a product called WD-40. The blue and yellow WD-40 can has a variety of uses, but most often we used it to quiet squeaky door hinges.

Though I had used the WD-40 I didn't know what it meant. I discovered WD-40 means "Water Displacement 40th Attempt." It took the scientists 39 times before they perfected it. On the 40th try it was perfected. Never give up! You are one try away from success.

DAY 89

Give and it shall be given unto you
good measure, pressed down, shaken together and running over
Luke 6:38

There are two bodies of water in the middle east; the Dead Sea and the Sea of Galilee. The Sea of Galilee is teaming and thriving with life. The Dead Sea on the other hand is lifeless and nothing thrives or survives there.

The difference is the Dead Sea only takes in water and never releases it. As a result it is stagnant and lifeless. But the Sea of Galilee not only takes in water but it also releases water as well. So there is a constant receiving and releasing.

DAY 90

More than that, we rejoice in our sufferings,
knowing that suffering produces endurance,
and endurance produces character, and character produces hope

Romans 5:3-4

I have fond memories of our family gathering for holidays and special occasions. Though there was always someone taking pictures, on this occasion my uncle was taking pictures with a camera I had never seen before.

The camera was square with an accordion like lens. When he took a picture, he pulled the actual picture out from the side of the camera. When he pulled it out there was no picture on it yet.

He began to shake the picture vigorously. As he shook it the picture began to develop in his hand. The more he shook, the more the picture developed. What was gray and dreary was now a bright and beautiful picture. But the beautiful picture could not have been developed without the shaking.

Made in the USA
San Bernardino, CA
06 February 2017